Heritage Auction Galleries

Dallas, Texas

Presents

THE
JAMES C. RUSSO
COLLECTION

OF RUSSIAN & BRITISH
ROYAL OBJECTS

April 24, 2008

THIS COLLECTION IS
BEING SOLD WITHOUT
CONSIGNOR RESERVES

ALL LOTS WILL OPEN AT 50%
OF THE LOW ESTIMATE

HERITAGE HA.com
Auction Galleries

3500 Maple Avenue, 17th Floor
Dallas, Texas 75219 | 800-872-6467

CORPORATE OFFICERS
R. Steven Ivy, Co-Chairman
James L. Halperin, Co-Chairman
Gregory J. Rohan, President
Paul Minshull, Chief Operating Officer
Todd Imhof, Vice President

HA.com/FineArt

Tim Robson, Managing Director, Fine Arts
Ext. 1606 • Tim@HA.com

Norma Gonzalez, Vice President - Auction Operations
Ext. 1242 • Norma@HA.com

UNITED STATES COINS

HA.com/Coins
U.S. Coins

Leo Frese, Ext. 1294
Leo@HA.com

Charles Clifford, Ext. 1477
CharlesC@HA.com

Sam Foose, Ext. 1227
SamF@HA.com

Jim Jelinski, Ext. 1257
JimJ@HA.com

Katherine Kurachek, Ext. 1389
KKurachek@HA.com

David Lewis, Ext. 1520
DLewis@HA.com

David Lisot, Ext. 1303
DavidL@HA.com

Bob Marino, Ext. 1374
BobMarino@HA.com

David Mayfield, Ext. 1277
DavidM@HA.com

Mike Sadler, Ext. 1332
MikeS@HA.com

Doug Nyholm, Ext. 1598
DNyholm@HA.com

Eugene Nowell, Ext. 1517
EugeneN@HA.com

Dave Lindvall, Ext. 1231
David@HA.com

Jason Friedman, Ext. 1582
JasonF@HA.com

UNITED STATES COINS PRIVATE TREATY SALES

HA.com/Coins
Todd Imhof, Ext. 1313
Todd@HA.com

CURRENCY

HA.com/Currency
Paper Money

Len Glazer, Ext. 1390
Len@HA.com

Allen Mincho, Ext. 1327
Allen@HA.com

Dustin Johnston, Ext. 1302
Dustin@HA.com

Jim Fitzgerald, Ext. 1348
JimF@HA.com

Michael Moczalla, Ext. 1481
MichaelM@HA.com

WORLD COINS

HA.com/Coins
World Coins & Currencies

Warren Tucker, Ext. 1287
WTucker@HA.com

Scott Cordry, Ext. 1369
ScottC@HA.com

Harvey Gamer, Ext. 1676
HarveyG@HA.com

Cristiano Bierrenbach, Ext. 1661
CrisB@HA.com

TOKENS & MEDALS

HA.com/Coins

Harvey Gamer, Ext. 1676
HarveyG@HA.com

CIVIL WAR HISTORICAL MATERIAL

HA.com/Civil War
Artifacts, Documents and Memorabilia Related to the American Civil War

Gary Hendershott, Ext. 1182
GaryH@HA.com

Douglass Brown, Ext. 1165
DouglassB@HA.com

COMICS

HA.com/Comics
Comics, Original Comic Art and Related Memorabilia

Ed Jaster, Ext. 1288
EdJ@HA.com

Lon Allen, Ext. 1261
LonA@HA.com

Barry Sandoval, Ext. 1377
BarryS@HA.com

MUSIC & ENTERTAINMENT MEMORABILIA

HA.com/Entertainment
Stage-Worn Costumes, Records, Signed Photos & Memorabilia

Doug Norwine, Ext. 1452
DougN@HA.com

John Hickey, Ext. 1264
JohnH@HA.com

Jim Steele, Ext. 1328
JimSt@HA.com

POLITICAL MEMORABILIA & AMERICANA

HA.com/Americana
Historical & Pop Culture Americana, Vintage Toys, Presidential & Political Memorabilia, Buttons & Medals, Books & Manuscripts, First Editions and Collectible Autographs

Tom Slater, Ext. 1441
TomS@HA.com

Marsha Dixey, Ext. 1455
MarshaD@HA.com

John Hickey, Ext. 1264
JohnH@HA.com

Michael Riley, Ext. 1467
MichaelR@HA.com

RARE BOOKS & MANUSCRIPTS

HA.com/Americana
Books & Manuscripts

Sandra Palomino, Ext. 1107
SandraP@HA.com

James Gannon, Ext. 1609
JamesG@HA.com

Joe Fay, Ext. 1544
JoeF@HA.com

SPORTS COLLECTIBLES

HA.com/Sports
Sports Cards, Artifacts, Game-Used Jerseys & Equipment

Chris Ivy, Ext. 1319
CIvy@HA.com

Derek Grady, Ext. 1617
DerekG@HA.com

Phillip Aman, Ext. 1106
PhillipA@HA.com

Stephen Carlisle, Ext. 1292
StephenC@HA.com

Mike Gutierrez, Ext. 1183
MikeG@HA.com

Lee Iskowitz, Ext. 1601
LeeI@HA.com

Mark Jordan, Ext. 1187
MarkJ@HA.com

Jonathan Scheier, Ext. 1314
JonathanS@HA.com

VINTAGE MOVIE POSTERS

HA.com/MoviePosters
Posters, Lobby Cards, and Hollywood Ephemera

Grey Smith, Ext. 1367
GreySm@HA.com

Bruce Carteron, Ext. 1551
BruceC@HA.com

CORPORATE & INSTITUTIONAL COLLECTIONS/VENTURES

Jared Green, Ext. 1279
Jared@HA.com

FINE ART

HA.com/FineArt
Impressionist, Old Masters and Contemporary Drawings, Paintings, Sculpture and Photography

Edmund P. Pillsbury, Ph.D., Ext. 1533
EPP@HA.com

Tim Robson, Ext. 1606
Tim@HA.com

Kathleen Guzman, Ext. 1672
KathleenG@HA.com

Ed Jaster, Ext. 1288
EdJ@HA.com

Christine Carmody, Ext. 1521
ChristineC@HA.com

Courtney Case, Ext. 1293
CourtneyC@HA.com

NATURAL HISTORY

David Herskowitz, Ext. 1610
DavidH@HA.com

PHOTOGRAPHY

Lorraine Davis, Ext. 1714
LorraineD@HA.com

RUSSIAN ART

Douglass Brown, Ext. 1165
DouglassB@HA.com

AMERICAN INDIAN ART

Delia Sullivan, Ext. 1343
DeliaS@HA.com

ART OF THE AMERICAN WEST & TEXAS ART

HA.com/TexasArt

Michael Duty, Ext. 1712
MichaelD@HA.com

ILLUSTRATION ART/ PHOTOGRAPHY

HA.com/FineArt
Pinups and Illustration Art

Ed Jaster, Ext. 1288
EdJ@HA.com

DECORATIVE ARTS

HA.com/FineArt
Sculpture, European & American Silver Antique Furniture, Art Glass & Ceramics

Michael Wolf, Ext. 1541
MWolf@HA.com

Tim Rigdon, Ext. 1119
TimR@HA.com

Meredith Meuwly, Ext. 1631
MeredithM@HA.com

JEWELRY & TIMEPIECES

HA.com/Jewelry
Jewelry & Timepieces

Jill Burgum, Ext. 1697
JillB@HA.com

MEDIA RELATIONS

Marketing and Public Relations

Kelley Norwine, Ext. 1583
KelleyN@HA.com

CREDIT DEPARTMENT

Marti Korver, Ext 1248
Marti@HA.com

Eric Thomas, Ext. 1241
EricT@HA.com

WIRING INSTRUCTIONS

Bank Information:
JP Morgan Chase Bank, N.A.
270 Park Avenue, New York, NY 10017
Account Name:
Heritage Numismatic Auctions
Master Account
ABA Number: 021000021
Account Number: 1884827674
Swift Code: CHASUS33

THE JAMES C. RUSSO COLLECTION OF RUSSIAN AND BRITISH ROYAL OBJECTS

April 24, 2008 | DALLAS, TEXAS

Heritage Auction Galleries | Design District Annex | 1518 Slocum St. | Dallas, Texas 75219

LOT VIEWING

London, England
April 2-3, 2008 | 9:30 AM-5:30 PM
April 4, 2008 | 9:30 AM-1:30 PM
Reception April 2 | 5:30PM-7:30PM
Pushkin House
5A Bloomsbury Square, London WC1A 2TA
+44 (0)20 7269 9770
www.pushkinhouse.org.uk

New York, New York
April 16-17, 2008 | 10:00 AM-6:00 PM
April 18, 2008 | 10:00 AM-2:00 PM
Reception April 16 | 6:00PM-8:00PM
Synod of Bishops of the Russian Orthodox
Church Outside of Russia
75 E. 93rd St., New York, NY 10128
(212) 534-1601
www.russianorthodoxchurch.ws/english/

Dallas, Texas
April 22-23, 2008 | 9:00 AM-5:00 PM CT
April 24, 2008 | 9:00 AM-12:00 PM CT
Reception April 22 | 6:00PM-8:00PM CT
Heritage Auction Galleries
Design District Annex
1518 Slocum St., Dallas, TX 75207
(214) 528-3500 | www.HA.com/FineArt

PREVIEW RECEPTION
Heritage Auction Galleries' Design District Annex,
1518 Slocum St., Dallas, TX 75207
Tuesday, April 22, 6:00 – 8:00 PM CT

CUSTOMER SERVICE
Direct Customer Service Line: 866.835.3243
For outside U.S., dial 001-214-409-1150

FAX BIDDING
Deadline: Wednesday, April 23, 2008
By 12:00 PM CT
Fax: 214.409.1425

INTERNET BIDDING
HA.com/FineArt | Bid@HA.com

Bidding closes at 10:00 PM CT
the evening before the auction

BID LIVE ON THE INTERNET AT HA.com

LIVE PHONE BIDDING
Customer Service: 866.835.3243
For outside U.S., dial 001-214-409-1150
Must be arranged on or before
Wednesday, April 23, 2008
By 5:00 PM CT

AUCTION SESSIONS

Session I – Russian
Thursday, April 24, 2008
10:00 AM CT, Lots 36001-36070

Session II - British & Continental
Thursday, April 24, 2008
12:00 PM CT, Lots 36071 -36247

Lots are sold at an approximate rate of 75 lots per hour, but it is not uncommon to sell 60 to 100 lots per hour.

This auction is subject to a 19.5% Buyer's Premium.

AUCTION RESULTS
Immediately available at: HA.com/FineArt

LOT SETTLEMENT AND PICK UP
Available immediately following each session or
Weekdays, 9:00 AM - 5:00 PM CT, by appointment only.
Third-party shipping applies for all shipped items;
contact client services at (866) 835-3243/214-409-1150

AUCTIONEERS
Kathleen Guzman 16142; Samuel Foose 11727; Robert Korver 13754; John Petty 13740; Ed Griffith 16343; Bob Merrill 13408; Mike Sadler 16129; Scott Peterson 13256; Andrea Voss 16406; Jacob Walker 16413

Heritage World Headquarters

HERITAGE HA.com
Auction Galleries

Direct Client Service Line: Toll Free 1.866.835.3243
3500 Maple Avenue, 17th Floor, Dallas, Texas 75219-3941
214.528.3500 | 800.872.6467 | 214.443.8425 (fax)

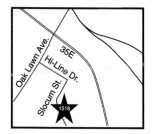

Heritage Design District Annex

THIS AUCTION IS PRESENTED AND CATALOGUED BY HERITAGE AUCTIONS, INC.
Catalogued by: Marie Betteley - Consultant; Kathleen Guzman; Professor David H. Schimmelpennick van der Oye - Historical Advisor
Edited by: Carrie Hunnicutt, Courtney E. Kennedy, Meredith Meuwly, Tim Robson, Lindsay Walton
Production and Design: Mary Hermann, Tim Hose, Matt Pegues, Chris Rodriguez, Mandy Wynne
Catalog and Internet Imaging: Keith Annis, Bryan Buchanan, Nina Castro, Crystal Hartmann, Tim Hose,
Darnell McCown, Roy Richardson, Brenna Wilson
Project Manager: Lindsay Walton; Operations Support: Abel Privado, Britt Barnstone, Jon Brotherton,
Royce Cornelison, Kay Cross, Jennifer Hill, Gerald King, Mairead Lamb

Steve Ivy
CEO
Co-Chairman
of the Board

Jim Halperin
Co-Chairman
of the Board

Greg Rohan
President

Paul Minshull
Chief Operating Officer

Edmund P. Pillsbury, Ph.D.
Chairman

Tim Robson
Managing Director

Kathleen Guzman
Senior Auctioneer

Douglass Brown Ph.D.
Russian Art Specialist

Marie Betteley
Consultant

FINE AND DECORATIVE ARTS DEPARTMENT

As an advisor to the State Hermitage Museum, I've been to Saint Petersburg countless times in recent years. Yet on every visit, I can't help being overwhelmed by the richness of the art commissioned by the Imperial family. Not only did Peter the Great establish Saint Petersburg as Russia's "Window to the West" in the early eighteenth century, he founded major academies and workshops to hire and train qualified artists and artisans and employed foreign and other agents to assemble one of the most impressive repositories of world art. His successors, in particular Catherine the Great, vastly expanded these endeavors, laying the groundwork for a collection that quickly rivaled, if not surpassed, those of Vienna, Paris, London, and older capitals of Europe.

It is no surprise that Russia has occupied such an important place in the minds of serious collectors of art. Its Romanov rulers were among the most lavish and enlightened patrons, while Russia's master-craftsmen created jewelry and porcelain coveted by royalty throughout the world. No country has used culture more effectively to promote its national interests. Even the most ordinary object bearing the inscription of some member of the ruling Romanovs or their extensive court assumes an aura of grandeur—and glamour.

An exquisite testimony of this legacy exists in the group of objects so enthusiastically and passionately assembled over the past two decades by the New Jersey native Jim Russo. With his partner Tony Cointreau, of the Cointreau liqueur family, Jim has selected from many of the best galleries and other sources a unique collection of royal artifacts ranging from a rare Fabergé silver desk clock that Czar Alexander III presented to his wife Maria Fedorovna for their 25th wedding anniversary in 1891 to a vintage bottle of 1961 Dom Perignon champagne ordered for the wedding breakfast of Princess Diana and Prince Charles – one of the few bottles that Diana saved herself.

The mission of Jim Russo has been a noble one. He has sought objects of beauty that preserve precious moments in the lives of their privileged owners. Every object bears a story: sometimes it is a very familiar one that was staged publicly for all the world to see, while other times, the tale is intensely private and virtually undocumented save for the object itself. These beautifully-crafted works offer glimpses into the character of their regal owners but also document a period of history that seems to be fast disappearing from memory save the brief excitement created by the engagement and fairy-tale wedding of one of the twentieth century's true superstars, Princess Diana.

While Jim Russo and Tony Cointreau could continue to expand and refine this extraordinary collection, they have chosen a higher path. They wish to embark upon a new chapter in their lives, devoted this time to philanthropy. The proceeds from the sale of the Princess Diana objects from their collection will help educate needy children around the world. Their resolve to effect change in the lives of the less fortunate is such that their legacy as philanthropists may one day match that of their remarkable gift as discerning collectors of the finest royal artifacts from the past two centuries.

Heritage Auction Galleries is privileged to have the honor of offering this unique opportunity to serious collectors. We must thank Jim Russo as well as Tony Cointreau for their trust and confidence in representing their collection. We are also deeply grateful to them for generously providing the information essential to the preparation of this catalog which was so carefully documented by Marie Betteley, a respected New York antique jewelry dealer who specializes in Russian antiques.

Edmund P. Pillsbury, Ph.D.
Chairman of Fine Arts
Heritage Auction Galleries

NOBLE MISSION

A SIMPLE MUG INSPIRED JIM RUSSO TO GATHER SOME OF THE WORLD'S MOST IMPORTANT ROYAL ARTIFACTS. NOW, HIS UNPARALLELED COLLECTION IS BEING OFFERED AT AUCTION.

IT WAS A THOUGHTFUL GIFT. A FRIEND knew Jim Russo liked England and so he gave Russo a porcelain mug with an image of King Edward VII, who ruled the country from 1901 until his death in 1910. "I thought, 'This is interesting,' and I started reading about Edward VII. The passion," Russo says, "evolved from there."

Twenty years later, the New Jersey native and former record-label promoter holds one of the world's most important collections of royal artifacts. "Over the years, I've always collected not just objects, but objects with a story or history behind them," Russo says. "I see it as collecting moments in time."

Those moments include a rare Imperial Russian Fabergé silver desk clock that Czar Alexander III presented to his wife Maria Fedorovna for their 25th wedding anniversary; a Czar Alexander I diamond and enamel Imperial presentation bracelet with 110 diamonds weighing approximately 20 carats; and a vintage bottle of 1961 Dom Perignon champagne, labeled for the wedding breakfast of Princess Diana and Prince Charles, dated July 29, 1981 – one of the few bottles that Diana saved for herself.

"Jim has always been extremely interested in the history of each piece, the background," says Marie

Empress Alexandra

Russian Imperial Porcelain Empress Alexandra Easter Egg with Stand. Estimate: $20,000-$30,000

Betteley, a New York antique jewelry dealer who specializes in Russian antiques. "That diamond-encrusted Alexander bracelet ... I've never seen a better piece of Russian jewelry. But Jim would not buy things just because they had a diamond or an imperial monogram. He bought things because he liked them and he knew what they were."

In addition to collecting, Russo has a new passion: helping educate needy children around the world, a passion sparked by a 2006 visit overseas with his partner Tony Cointreau, of the Cointreau liqueur family.

Heritage's James C. Russo Collection of Royal Artifacts auction is scheduled for April 24, 2008.

You worked for Capitol Records in the 1960s. How did that come about?

Russo: I saw an ad in *The New York Times.* I went and interviewed for the job and got it. It was while working there that I met Tony. He was a singer who performed in clubs and arenas around the world. I became his manager, and we've been together 41 years now. We were a team in every aspect

Interview with Jim Russo

Does it surprise you that you collect so extensively,
or have you always been a collector?

Russo: There is absolutely nothing in my genes that
would have led to my collecting. Nothing. Certainly not anything to do with royalty. I'm from a small town in New Jersey,
and I never knew any collectors when I was growing up. My
collecting just evolved when a friend who knew I loved London brought me back a porcelain mug with a picture of King
Edward VII. Soon afterwards I went to London and started
acquiring more royal collectibles. I didn't care which country
they came from – it was the history that I loved, and I read
obsessively to learn more about it.

And you never collected anything
before that, even as a child?

Russo: No. Collecting was so far from my mind. I did get
little rings from cereal boxes, like a lot of kids of my genera-
tion. But, no. I didn't have the fascination for history that I
have now. It all developed later as the collection evolved and I
began to look for items that had a story behind them. That's
how I tried to build my collection ... a moment in time, a moment in history.

Your collection has numerous royal "presentation"
items – presentation bracelets, presentation desk
clocks, presentation Easter eggs, presentation
brooches. Can you talk about that? What's the
history behind royal presentation gifts?

Russo: Royalty would present gifts to their families or
visiting diplomats or dignitaries. I have a beautiful piece, a
brooch and earrings, originally on a box that was given by
Alexander I to a British rear admiral. Gifts were made specifically for presentations and there weren't many made – some
were one-of-a-kind. I have an extraordinary silver clock given
by Alexander III to his wife Empress Maria Fedorovna for
their 25th wedding anniversary. It was made by Fabergé and
has the Roman numeral XXV on top. Their whole life is
written on that clock. Instead of numbers for the hours, his
nickname for her is spelled out in Cyrillic on one side. On the
other side are the first initials of the name of each of their children. The names of all their homes were engraved on the front
of the clock, and at the bottom of the clock is the date October
28, the day they were married. It's the epitome of what I love.

Interview by *HECTOR CANTU*
Russo and living room photographs by *DAVID PALER*

RUSSIAN

SESSION ONE | APRIL 24, 2008 | 10 AM CT

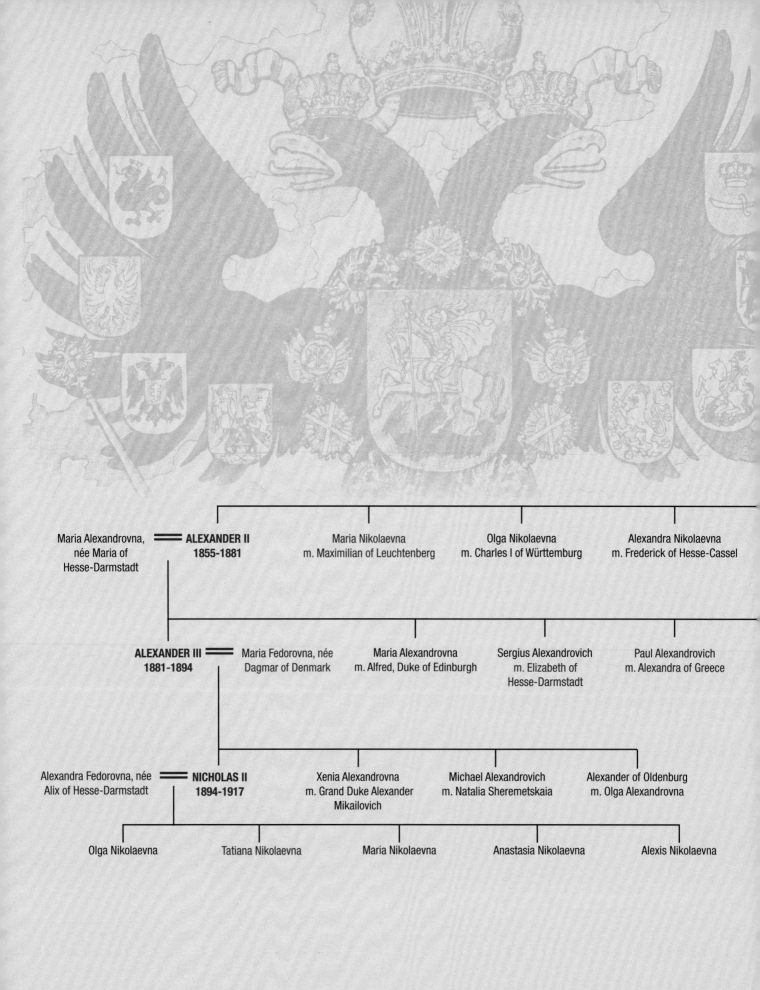

Maria Alexandrovna, née Maria of Hesse-Darmstadt ═══ **ALEXANDER II 1855-1881**

Maria Nikolaevna m. Maximilian of Leuchtenberg

Olga Nikolaevna m. Charles I of Württemburg

Alexandra Nikolaevna m. Frederick of Hesse-Cassel

ALEXANDER III 1881-1894 ═══ Maria Fedorovna, née Dagmar of Denmark

Maria Alexandrovna m. Alfred, Duke of Edinburgh

Sergius Alexandrovich m. Elizabeth of Hesse-Darmstadt

Paul Alexandrovich m. Alexandra of Greece

Alexandra Fedorovna, née Alix of Hesse-Darmstadt ═══ **NICHOLAS II 1894-1917**

Xenia Alexandrovna m. Grand Duke Alexander Mikailovich

Michael Alexandrovich m. Natalia Sheremetskaia

Alexander of Oldenburg m. Olga Alexandrovna

Olga Nikolaevna

Tatiana Nikolaevna

Maria Nikolaevna

Anastasia Nikolaevna

Alexis Nikolaevna

The Russian Royal Family

Colored names indicate those with items in the sale.

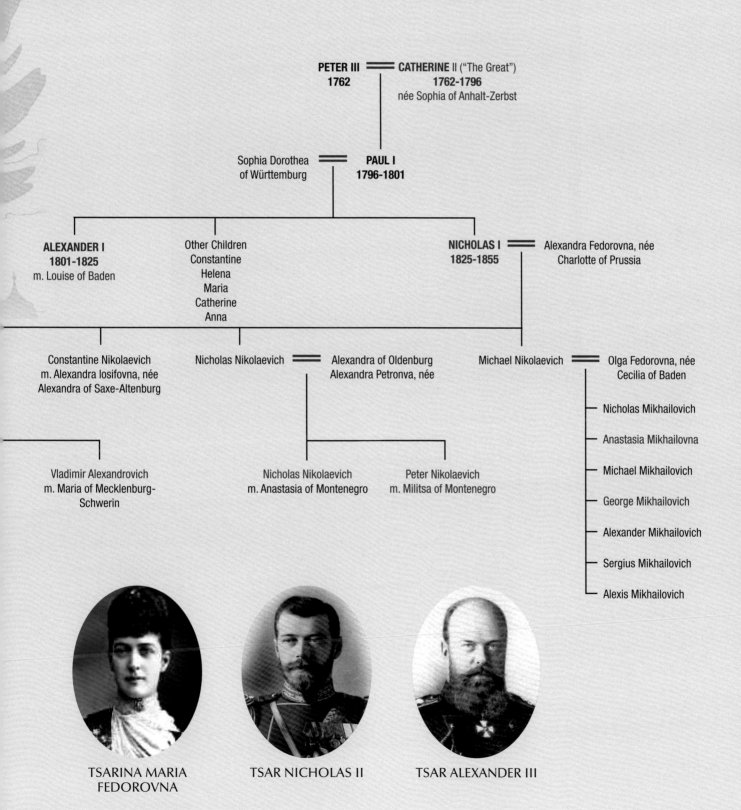

PETER III
1762

CATHERINE II ("The Great")
1762-1796
née Sophia of Anhalt-Zerbst

Sophia Dorothea
of Württemburg

PAUL I
1796-1801

ALEXANDER I
1801-1825
m. Louise of Baden

Other Children
Constantine
Helena
Maria
Catherine
Anna

NICHOLAS I
1825-1855

Alexandra Fedorovna, née
Charlotte of Prussia

Constantine Nikolaevich
m. Alexandra Iosifovna, née
Alexandra of Saxe-Altenburg

Nicholas Nikolaevich

Alexandra of Oldenburg
Alexandra Petronva, née

Michael Nikolaevich

Olga Fedorovna, née
Cecilia of Baden

Nicholas Mikhailovich

Anastasia Mikhailovna

Michael Mikhailovich

George Mikhailovich

Alexander Mikhailovich

Sergius Mikhailovich

Alexis Mikhailovich

Vladimir Alexandrovich
m. Maria of Mecklenburg-
Schwerin

Nicholas Nikolaevich
m. Anastasia of Montenegro

Peter Nikolaevich
m. Militsa of Montenegro

TSARINA MARIA
FEDOROVNA

TSAR NICHOLAS II

TSAR ALEXANDER III

36001

Repoussé Silver-Plated Copper Portrait of Catherine the Great

Circa 1770, signed JB Nini F after an original terracotta by Jean Baptiste Nini (1717-86)

Circular in the form of a portrait medallion, depicting the bust of Catherine the Great, facing right, the silver insignia *E II (Ekaterina II)* in Russian for Empress Catherine II (r. 1762-1796), below Romanov crown mounted separately above, both mounted on a rectangular red velvet frame within silvered outer border-the central portrait-6 1/2 in. diam.; the frame-11 x 9 3/8 in.

Catherine II "the Great" (1729-1796)

Fully deserving the epithet "Great", the former Princess Sophie of Anhalt-Zerbst remains one of the most remarkable figures in Russia's colorful past. The correspondent of some of the Age of Reason's brightest minds, conqueror of vast new lands, and coquette of gallant guardsmen, Empress Catherine II was the archetypal enlightened despot. The three decades of her rule at the eighteenth century's close completed the westward journey on which Peter the Great had set Russia in its opening years.

Literature:

For an original medallion of Catherine the Great by Nini, see, lot 214, *Catalogue des Tableaux, Dessins, Aquarelles, Gouaches, Objects d'Art et d'ameublement du XVIIème Siècle composant La collection de Mr. Gustave Mühlbacher* (Paris, 1907), Galerie George Petit, 8 Rue de Sèze, Paris.

Provenance:

Purchased from A la Vieille Russie

Estimate: $3,000 - $5,000

36002

Gold and Enamel Egg Pendant

20th century

Of polished gold, decorated with enameled black and white enameled initial *N* below a red enameled crown, the opening on the top unscrews, with vacant interior, stamped on suspension ring- 1 3/4 in.

Provenance:

Purchased from Sheldon Shapiro, London

Estimate: $2,500 - $3,500

36003

Gold and Gem-Set Egg Pendant

20th century, stamped with spurious Fabergé marks

Of polished gold, decorated with rose-cut diamonds, sapphires, rubies, set within stars, a fly and a fleur-de-lis, top opens (unscrews) to reveal vacant compartment set with images of Tsar Nicholas II and Tsarina Alexandra- 1 in.

Provenance:

Purchased from Sheldon Shapiro, London

Estimate: $2,500 - $3,500

The Russo Collection is being sold without consignor reserves. All lots will open at 50% of the low estimate.

Session One, Auction #5003 | Thursday, April 24, 10:00 AM CT   5

36004

Russian Brass Imperial Presentation Easter Egg

Late 19th century

A watchcase designed as a brass egg divided vertically into two halves, opening from the top with a pushpiece and suspension ring, revealing vacant interiors, the exterior of one side applied with a Russian Imperial double-headed eagle, the reverse with a red and white enamel *XB*, the Cyrillic initials for the Russian Easter Proclamation *Khristos Voskrese (Christ is Risen),* attached to a large oval link brass chain-the egg-3 1/2 in. long

Provenance:

Purchased from A la Vieille Russie

Estimate: $1,000 - $2,000

RARE RUSSIAN EMPRESS ALEXANDRA
IMPERIAL PORCELAIN EASTER EGG

36005

Rare Russian Empress Alexandra Imperial Porcelain Easter Egg

By the Imperial Porcelain Factory, St. Petersburg, circa 1910

Decorated with the interlaced Cyrillic monogram *A F* in two-toned gold for Empress Alexandra Fedorovna (1872-1918), wife of Tsar Nicholas II, on cobalt blue ground with gilded openings, fitted with original silk ribbon- 3 1/2 in high, in red leather presentation box. Together with card inscribed *Prince Vladimir Galitzine, Objets d'Art 202 Berkeley St, Picadilly W 1*

Alexandra Fedorovna (1872-1918)

The consort of Russia's last Tsar, Alexandra entered the world as a princess in the small German principality of Hesse-Darmstadt. Her marriage to Nicholas II in 1894 proved to be a successful match, but domestic bliss was severely tested by the hemophilia of her son, the Tsarevich Alexis. Acting under orders from their leader, Vladimir Lenin, the Bolsheviks shot Alexandra along with her family in 1918.

For a similar egg in red see Tamara Kudriavtseva and Harold A. Whitbeck, *Russian Imperial Porcelain Easter Eggs* (London, 2001), p. 51.

Provenance:

Christie's, New York

Estimate: $20,000 - $30,000

The Russo Collection is being sold without consignor reserves. All lots will open at 50% of the low estimate.

Session One, Auction #5003 | Thursday, April 24, 10:00 AM CT   9

36006

Imperial Russian Gilt Metal Easter Egg

Third quarter of the 19th century

Of typical form, hinged and fitted with pushpiece within suspension ring, the exterior of one half applied with *Khristos* in Cyrillic, the other half with *Voskrese*, for the Russian Orthodox Easter greeting, *Christ is Risen*, opening to reveal an oval portrait of a lady facing left said to be that of Russian Empress Maria Fedorovna (1847-1928), wife of Tsar Alexander III, wearing somber clothes, the frame lifts on a hinge to reveal vacant compartment, with another vacant compartment opposite, lined in moiré silk-length of egg-4 in.

Provenance:
Purchased from St. Petersburg Shop, Paris

Estimate: $2,000 - $3,000

36007

Russian Empress Alexandra Fedorovna Imperial Porcelain Easter Egg

By the Imperial Porcelain Factory, St. Petersburg, 1914-1917

Decorated with the entwined openwork Cyrillic initials *A F* for Russian Empress Alexandra Fedorovna (1872-1918), wife of Tsar Nicholas II, in a Slavic interlaced style, the cipher in gold and gray below a toned gold Romanov crown on white ground, with an opening on each end to accommodate a ribbon or cord (now missing)-2 3/4 in. high

Estimate: $1,500 - $2,000

RUSSIAN EMPRESS MARIA FEDOROVNA
IMPERIAL PORCELAIN EASTER EGG

36008

Rare Russian Empress Maria Fedorovna Imperial Porcelain Easter Egg

By the Imperial Porcelain Factory, St. Petersburg, late 19th century

Decorated with the interlaced Cyrillic monogram *M F* in two-toned gold for Empress Maria Fedorovna, wife of Tsar Alexander III, on painted ox-blood glazed ground intentionally fading to faint light blue on the ends- 4 in. long, with later silk ribbon

For centuries in Russia, Easter eggs of all sizes and materials were exchanged on Orthodox Easter as symbols of the Resurrection of Christ. Across the empire, eggs decorated homes, churches, and palaces, usually suspended from a ribbon or braided cord around religious icons.

The rarest and most valuable porcelain eggs are those with the Imperial ciphers. These were made in St. Petersburg's Imperial Porcelain Factory, which was founded by Empress Elizabeth in 1741. Red was the preferred traditional Easter color. While red glazes first appeared in French and Viennese porcelain factories, only the Russian Imperial Porcelain Factory used the glaze to decorate eggs. Experiments were carried out by K. F. Klever (1854-after 1910) who achieved the *sang de boeuf* tone with the aid of copper compounds, after well-known Chinese glazes. For another example in the Hermitage Museum see *Imperial Easter Eggs* (Copenhagen, 1994), fig 89.

Maria Fedorovna (1847-1928)

Born Princess Dagmar of Denmark, and the younger sister of Edward VII's consort, Maria Fedorovna had initially been betrothed to Tsar Alexander II's eldest son, Tsarevich Nicholas Alexandrovich. When he grew mortally ill, Nicholas commanded his younger brother Alexander to marry her. An outgoing woman of great charm, Empress Maria proved an ideal match for her forbidding mate, Tsar Alexander III. She survived both her husband's death and the Revolution of 1917, and ended her days in her native Denmark.

Provenance:

Purchased from A la Vieille Russie

Estimate: $12,000 - $15,000

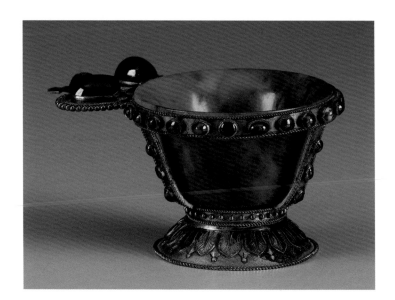

36009

Russian Nephrite Gem-Set Charka with Romanov Crown Handle

In the style of ancient Muscovy, the small hardstone cup on a gilt metal spreading base decorated with a border of laurel leaves, enclosed by bands set with alternating cabochon rubies and sapphires, the flat shaped handle in the form of the Romanov crown set with two cabochon garnets centering a sapphire-1 ¾ in. high

Provenance:

Purchased from St. Petersburg Shop, Paris

Estimate: $400 - $600

The Russo Collection is being sold without consignor reserves. All lots will open at 50% of the low estimate.

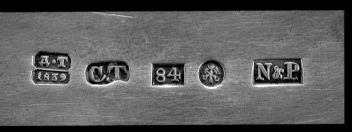

Imperial Russian Silver Toilet Box from the Wedding Service of Grand Duchess Maria Nikolaevna and Maximilian, Duke of Leuchtenberg

Marked Nicholls & Plincke, St. Petersburg, 1839, by Carl Johan Tegelsten, assaymaster Dmitri Tverskoy, stamped on base and cover

Oval with gilt interior, the shaped hinged cover with ovolo-bracket border, resting on double lion-paw feet, the front with crowned initials of the Grand Duchess within a cartouche, the back with Romanov Imperial double-headed eagle below crown-10 1/8 x 4 3/4 in.

Nicholas I's eldest daughter, Grand Duchess Maria Nikolaevna (1819-1876), married Maximilian de Beauharnais, Duke of Leuchtenberg (1817-1852) in 1839. Her union with the grandson of Napoleon's wife, Josephine, was severely criticized by many Russians, who had memories of the Corsican upstart's invasion 27 years earlier in 1812. Nevertheless, the couple made their home in Russia, and Nicholas I granted Maximilian the title of Imperial Highness.

36011

Large Russian-Style Silvered and Enameled Ormolu Paperknife

20th century

The handle decorated with pearl-set cipher of Tsar Nicholas II on blue *guilloché* ground set with two small diamonds on either side, surmounted by a Romanov crown, the blade engraved *POMNI* in Russian-15 in. long, in fitted leather silk-lined box

Provenance:

St. Petersburg Shop, Paris

Estimate: $2,000 - $2,500

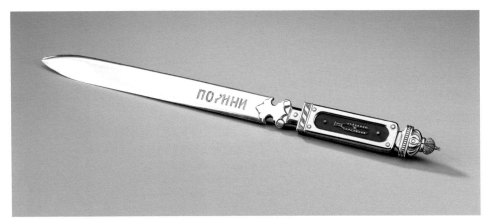

36012

Imperial Russian Silver Souvenir Cigarette Case

Marked Moscow, 1899-1908

The case overall decorated with pebbled pattern with rounded corners, the cover applied with three clusters of gold initials the central one larger and below a gold coronet, the interior with dedication inscription in Russian and dated *1901*-4 1/4 x 3 in.

Estimate: $800 - $1,200

The Russo Collection is being sold without consignor reserves. All lots will open at 50% of the low estimate.

Session One, Auction #5003 | Thursday, April 24, 10:00 AM CT   15

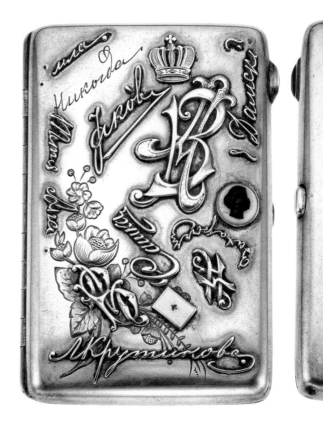

36013

Imperial Russian Silver and Enameled Souvenir Cigarette Case

Marked Moscow, 1880

Profusely decorated with gold ciphers, a crown, signatures, and ace of spades in white enamel, the reverse applied with a white enamel pallet and silver brush, an inscription in Russian and applied with the name *Ella* in gold-4 x 2 3/4 in.

Provenance:

Purchased from Manhattan Art & Antiques Center, New York

Estimate: $1,000 - $1,500

36014

Russian Karelian Birchwood Imperial Presentation Cigarette Case

Circa 1890

The cover applied with the conjoined Cyrillic initials of Grand Duke Nikolai Nikolaevich (grandson of Emperor Nicholas I), below a Romanov crown in silver, with spine to accommodate a tinder cord (missing), the top with hinged match compartment and exterior match strike- 3 3/4 x 2 5/8 in.

He was the most admired man in the army, not only an old fashioned soldier, but deeply Slav. His whole being exuded a fierce energy. His incisive measured speed, flashing eyes and quick, nervous movements, hard, steel-trap mouth and gigantic stature personify imperious and impetuous audacity. - Maurice Paléologue.

Grand Duke Nikolai Nikolaevich (1856-1929) was the uncle of Tsar Nicholas II and Commander-in-Chief of the Russian Army at the outbreak of World War I. He began his career as young officer during the Turkish War (1877-78), where he was awarded a Saint George's Cross. He went on to command a Guards Hussar Regiment and eventually the entire Imperial Guard. After the Revolution, the Grand Duke went on to the Crimea, although he was not involved in the Civil War. In 1919 the British Navy evacuated him on the *H.M.S. Nelson* along with the Dowager Empress, Maria Fedorovna.

Provenance:

Purchased from Sheldon Shapiro, London

Estimate: $2,000 - $3,000

36015

Imperial Russian Silver Souvenir Cigarette Case

Marked Ivan Saltykov, Moscow, 1885, assaymaster Victor Savinkov, 84

Rectangular, of reeded design, the hinged cover applied with a Russian gold double-headed eagle in the center and the crowned ciphers of Tsars Alexander I (r. 1801-1825) and Nicholas II (r. 1896-1917) with additional ribbon-tied red stone motif, with hidden match and tinder cord compartment- 4 1/8 x 2 1/2 x 3/4 in.

Provenance:

Purchased from Marie E. Betteley, New York

Estimate: $3,000 - $4,000

The Russo Collection is being sold without consignor reserves. All lots will open at 50% of the low estimate.

Session One, Auction #5003 | Thursday, April 24, 10:00 AM CT   17

Fabergé Imperial Presentation Silver Cigarette Case

Workmaster August Hollming, St. Petersburg, 1899-1908

The silver case set with a gold Romanov crown above the cipher of Grand Duchess Alexandra Iosifovna (1830-1911), daughter of Joseph, Duke of Saxe-Altenburg, wife of Constantine Nikolaevich, second son of Tsar Nicholas I and Alexandra Fedorovna, with a cabochon moonstone thumbpiece-2 ¼ x 3 ½ in.

Fabergé workmaster, August Hollming (1854-1913)

Born in Loppi, Finland, August Fredrik Hollming became a registered goldsmith in St. Petersburg in 1876. He first opened a workshop at 35 Kazanskaya Street and in 1900, moved into the Fabergé shop at 24 Bolshaya Morskaya Street. There, as workmaster, he specialized in gold and enameled jewelry, miniature egg pendants, and boxes. Fabergé cigarette cases were usually entrusted to either headworkmaster Henrik Wigström or August Hollming. One of the finest examples of Hollming's *oeuvre* is an imperial presentation box in diamonds and yellow *guilloché* enamel in the Collection of H.M. the Queen Mother.

Provenance:

Purchased from Marie E. Betteley, New York

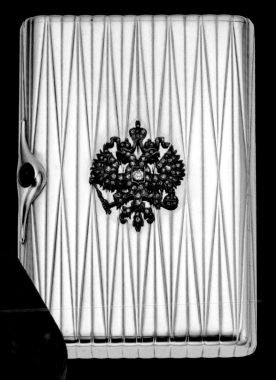

Russian Gold and Diamond Imperial Presentation Cigarette Case

Marked Carl Blank, St. Petersburg, 1908-17

Overall decorated with a tapering reeded pattern, the hinged cover applied in the center with a Russian double-headed eagle set with rose and antique-cut diamonds, with cabochon sapphire pushpiece-3 5/8 x 2 3/8 in.

In original red velvet fitted case stamped with a gold Imperial Russian double-headed eagle

Like many of Russia's finest jewelers, Carl Carlovich Blank was born in Finland and moved to St. Petersburg to learn his trade. He registered in the capital as a gold and silversmith and joined the renowned firm of Karl Hahn at 26 Nevskii Prospect, being made partner in 1911. Awarded the Imperial warrant at the end of the 19th century, the firm competed with Fabergé for Imperial commissions. Carl Blank won prizes for excellence at an exhibition in 1896 and won favor with the Imperial family by specializing in the diamond presentation gifts for the Russian Court.

Provenance:

Christie's, New York

36018

Brown Agate Cigarette Case with Diamond Double-Headed Eagle

20th century, unmarked

With rounded corners, the case of translucent, lightly banded agate applied with a Russian-style Imperial eagle set with single-cut diamonds and a tear-drop shaped cabochon ruby, mounted in silver (one diamond missing), its claws clutching a gold orb and scepter, fitted with a cabochon sapphire thumbpiece-3 1/2 in. long

For a cigarette case of similar inspiration formerly in the Frank Sinatra Collection, see Christies, New York, December 1, 1995, lot 54.

Provenance:

Purchased from St. Petersburg Shop, Paris

Estimate: $3,500 - $5,500

36019

Imperial Russian Enameled Silver-Gilt Romanov Tercentenary Cross of 1913

Stamped Moscow, 1908-17, maker's mark AO

Designed as a green, black, and white enameled cross, surmounted by the Crown of Monomakh, the reverse decorated with the inscription: *We Rule the Empire Through God*, with initials *M* for Michael and Cyrillic *N* for Nicholas II, for the first and last Romanov Tsar, with the Russian Coat of Arms and the dates *1613* and *1913*-2.6 in. long

The Tercentenary cross was presented to Orthodox Priests for exceptional merit and issued in memory of the 300th anniversary of the Romanov dynasty.

Provenance:

Purchased from A la Vieille Russie

Estimate: $2,000 - $3,000

A 19.5% Buyer's Premium applies to all lots.
Visit HA.com/FineArt to view scalable images and bid online.

RARE AND UNUSUAL FABERGE OXIDIZED GOLD CRUCIFIX
OF THE PROTOPRESBYTER (CONFESSOR) OF
TSAR ALEXANDER III AND MARIA FEDOROVNA

36020

Rare and Unusual Fabergé Oxidized Gold Crucifix of the Protopresbyter (Confessor) of Tsar Alexander III and Maria Fedorovna

Workmaster Erik Kollin, St. Petersburg, circa 1885, stamped 56 for 14k, and Fabergé in Cyrillic

Set with five garnet clusters of three pear-shaped bezel-set garnets and twenty-seven old mine-cut diamonds, the cross applied with the gold figure of Christ above *INRI*-6 in. long

The Protopresbyter was the highest-ranking white (married) cleric in Russia. At the end of the 19th century there were four priests who held this rank, including the head of the court clergy, who served as the personal confessor of the Russian Imperial family. White clergy wore the crucifix as opposed to the panagia (icon pendant) worn by the black (monastic) clergy.

Fabergé workmaster Erik Kollin

Born in Finland, Erik August Kollin (1836-1901) moved to St. Petersburg in 1858 where he registered as a goldsmith and worked with Fabergé workmaster August Holmström. Ten years later, Kollin became a master goldsmith and in 1870 opened his own workshop in the Imperial capital at 9 Kazanskaya, where he worked exclusively for Fabergé. He became headworkmaster of the Fabergé workshop and held that post until 1886. He is known for a series of Scythian jewelry recreations for which he received a Gold Medal at the Exhibition of Applied Arts in Nuremberg in 1885.

For another gold pectoral cross by Erik Kollin in the Bayerisches Nationalmuseum, see Geza von Habsburg, *Fabergé,* Munich, 1986, page 146, plate 134.

Provenance:
Purchased from A la Vieille Russie

Estimate: $60,000 - $90,000

The Russo Collection is being sold without consignor
reserves. All lots will open at 50% of the low estimate.

36021

Imperial Russian Enameled Silver Romanov Tercentenary Pendant in the Form of a Miniature Photo Album

Stamped St. Petersburg, 1908-17

The cover of the rectangular miniature book pendant enameled in royal blue, applied with a Russian Imperial double-headed eagle with dates *1613* and *1913*, containing images of all the Romanov sovereigns from the first, Tsar Michael Fedorovich (r. 1613-1645) and the last, Emperor Nicholas Alexandrovich (r. 1894-1917), along with images of Dowager Empress Maria Fedorovna, Empress Alexandra Fedorovna, the Tsarevich Grand Duke Alexei Nikolaevich-1 in. long

The Romanov Tercentenary marked the dynasty's final chapter. Ironically, despite his imminent demise, the last Tsar's popularity had never been greater, as the cheering masses during the 1913 celebrations revealed. A service in the Cathedral of Our Lady of Kazan in St. Petersburg was held in February, followed by numerous receptions at the Winter Palace and a lavish ball in honor of the Imperial Couple, Nicholas and Alexandra. To commemorate Russia's pre-Petrine past, the Tsarina wore the traditional *kokoshnik* headdress with a simple tunic. In May, the couple retraced the pilgrimage taken by Michael Fedorovich, the first Romanov Tsar, from his birthplace in Kostroma to the ancient capital of Moscow.

Provenance:

Purchased from A la Vieille Russie

Estimate: $2,500 - $3,500

36022

Imperial Russian Silver and Enamel Grand Duchess Tatiana Lady-in-Waiting Pendant

St. Petersburg, 1908-17

Shield-shaped, of deep blue enamel applied with the entwined initials *N T* for Grand Duchess Tatiana Nikolaevna, second child of Emperor Nicholas II, below a Romanov crown, the reverse engraved, with original sticker-1 1/2 in long, in original Imperial presentation box stamped *Edvard*

Nicholas and Alexandra's second daughter, Grand Duchess Tatiana Nikolaevna, was born in 1897. Tall, slender, with lush chestnut hair and a strong-willed yet elegant bearing, there was no mistaking her imperial blood. The Grand Duchess perished in Ekaterinburg a few weeks after her 21st birthday along with the rest of her family on orders of the new Bolshevik regime.

Provenance:

Purchased from A la Vieille Russie

Estimate: $2,500 - $3,500

36023

**Rare Russian Alexander I Diamond
and Enamel Ring**

Late 18th century, unmarked

Elliptical and curved to conform to the finger, the top
decorated with royal blue enamel, the center applied
with the monogram *A*, for Tsarevich Alexander
Pavlovich, future Tsar Alexander I of Russia (r. 1801-
1825) in rose diamonds, enhanced by a larger old
European-cut diamond, mounted in gold and silver-
top of ring-1 5/8 in.

Dating from circa 1780-1790, the larger diamond
on this ring is said to represent the cipher *I* in
anticipation of the future Tsar's coronation in 1801.

*Grand Duke Alexander Pavlovich, Future Tsar of
Russia*

As a grand duke, Alexander Pavlovich received the
best education possible under the supervision of
his doting grandmother, Catherine the Great, who
was not overly fond of the future Emperor Paul I,
Alexander's father. Raised in the tradition of the
Enlightenment by the Swiss *philosophe*, Frédéric-
César la Harpe, the handsome grand duke enjoyed
the reputation of a reformer, growing increasingly
popular as the despotic and demented ways of
his father thoroughly alienated his long-suffering
subjects.

Provenance:

Purchased from A la Vieille Russie

Estimate: $18,000 - $25,000

The Russo Collection is being sold without consignor
reserves. All lots will open at 50% of the low estimate.

Session One, Auction #5003 | Thursday, April 24, 10:00 AM CT   25

Gentleman's Enamel and Gold Ring

20th century

In the Russian style, applied with a gold Russian
imperial eagle on a blue enamel base within
enameled border

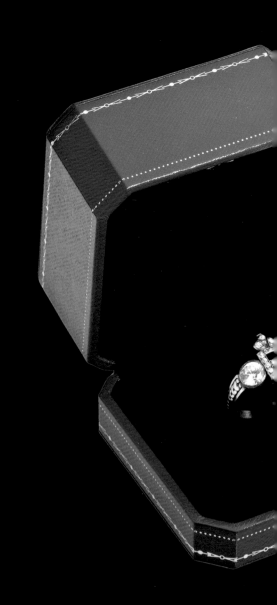

36025

Gentleman's Imperial Russian Nicholas II Ring

Circa 1900

A rare Russian 18k gold ring centered by an insignia
N II for Tsar Nicholas II in diamonds, flanked by two
antique pastes in bezel settings

George Mikhailovich (1863-1919)

Grand Duke George, grandson of Tsar Nicholas I, was
a boyhood friend of Nicholas II and accompanied
him on his World Tour in 1891. In Japan, he is said
to have saved the Tsarevich's life from a Samurai-
wielding policeman. In 1900, he married Princess
Marie Georgievna (1876-1940), the fifth child of King
George I of Greece and Olga Konstantinovna of
Russia. In 1919, George was killed by the Bolsheviks in
St. Petersburg.

Provenance:

From the private collection of the descendants of
Grand Duke George Mikhailovich (1863-1919).

Purchased from Marie E. Betteley, New York

Estimate: $5,000 - $7,000

Right: The Grand Duke at the Winter
Palace Costume Ball of 1903, dressed as a
17th-century *postel'nichii* (chamberlain).

36026

An Ivory Portrait Miniature of Nicholas II

20th century

A miniature on ivory of Nicholas II, Tsar of Russia (r. 1896-1917) in military uniform (facing viewer) signed with initials *GD,* within a tortoiseshell boulle frame- 5 ½ x 4 5/8 in.

Estimate: $2,000 - $3,000

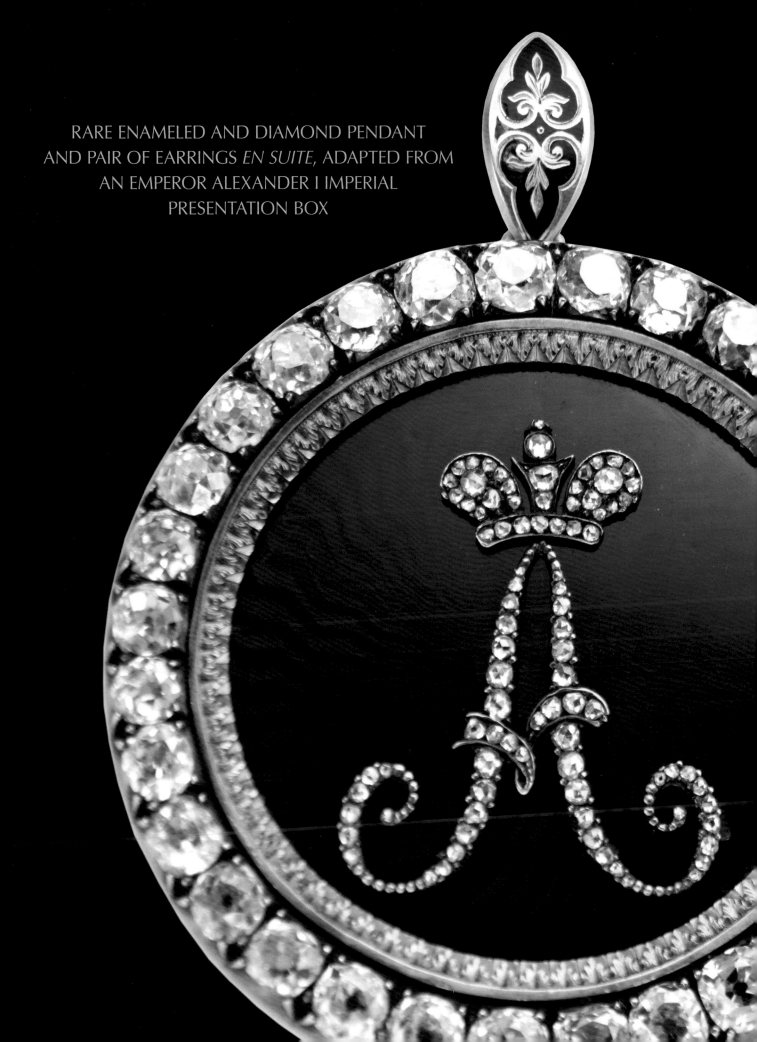

RARE ENAMELED AND DIAMOND PENDANT
AND PAIR OF EARRINGS *EN SUITE,* ADAPTED FROM
AN EMPEROR ALEXANDER I IMPERIAL
PRESENTATION BOX

A LA VIEILLE RUSSIE
781 FIFTH AVENUE
NEW YORK

This Locket
and a pair of Earrings
were made from a box
presented by
The Emperor Alexander of Russia
in 1812 to
R. Adml. Thomas Byam Martin
for the defence of Riga
and other services
in the Baltic

36027

Rare Enameled and Diamond Pendant and Pair of Earrings *en suite*, Adapted from an Emperor Alexander I Imperial Presentation Box

Mounted in England as a pendant and pair of earrings, early 19th century

The circular pendant designed as a royal blue *guilloché* enameled plaque inset with the crowned initial *A* for Emperor Alexander I of Russia, set with numerous rose diamonds, within a gold acanthus stiff-leaf border surrounded by thirty-one old mine-cut diamonds, the reverse inscribed *This locket and pair of earrings were made from a box presented by Emperor Alexander of Russia in 1812 to Adm'l Thomas Bijam Martin, for defence of Riga and other services in the Baltic*-attached to a retractable blue enamel and gold suspension ring-2 1/2 in. including ring

Each pendant earring designed as two pear-shaped diamonds on a royal blue enamel and gold base connected by a circular old mine-cut diamond, mounted in silver and gold-1 5/8 in. long-the suite in original blue velvet fitted box stamped *L Stoppard Goldsmiths & Jeweler to the Queen 63 Brook Street, Hanover Sq. London*

Total approximate weight of diamonds: 15.36 carats

Sir Thomas Byam Martin, G.C.B. (1773-1854) saw considerable action in the Baltic Sea during the allied effort against Napoleon. He had an illustrious career in the Royal Navy, winning promotions to Rear Admiral in 1811 and Admiral of the Fleet in 1815. After the return of peace, Sir Thomas served as Comptroller of the Navy from 1818 through 1831 and also sat in Parliament as member for Plymouth for 13 years, beginning in 1818.

Provenance:

Made from a box presented by Tsar Alexander I of Russia in 1812 to Rear Admiral Thomas Byam Martin, for actions in the Baltic during the Napoleonic wars.

Purchased from A la Vieille Russie

Estimate: $60,000 - $80,000

36028

Gentleman's Russian Silver Pocket Watch

Late 19th century

Hunter's case, the cover applied with a high-relief Imperial Romanov double-headed eagle, opening to reveal a white enamel dial with blue steel spade hands, Roman chapters with subsidiary seconds, and a second hand dial, signed *Pavel Buhre* in Cyrillic, with original Swiss 11 jewel nickel movement and platform lever escapement, stamped 875 silver inside dust cover, with engine turned back cover, attached to a later twisted rope chain-53 mm diam., the chain-16 in. long

Born into a family of watchmakers from Neuchâtel who settled in Russia in the 19th century, Pavel Buhre provided most of the watches commissioned by the Imperial Family during the reign of Nicholas II. In 1899, the firm received the title of Supplier to the Imperial Court.

Estimate: $400 - $600

The Russo Collection is being sold without consignor reserves. All lots will open at 50% of the low estimate.

Session One, Auction #5003 | Thursday, April 24, 10:00 AM CT   31

36029

Rare Russian Imperial Diamond Maid of Honor Decoration

By Karl Hahn, 1896-1911, unsigned, with inventory number

Designed as the conjoined initials *M A* for Dowager Empress Maria Fedorovna and Empress Alexandra Fedorovna, below a Romanov Crown set with diamonds, the scrolling terminals set with sapphires

Karl Hahn, Jeweler to the Imperial Court

Like Fabergé, Hahn was an important supplier to the Russian Imperial Court who also had the title of Court Jeweler. Based in St. Petersburg, the firm specialized in Court commissions: diamond orders and decorations, portrait badges, snuffboxes, jewels, and *objets d'art*. The firm closed in 1911.

Recipients of these diamond ciphers were young unmarried women of aristocratic background personally chosen by both the Empress and Dowager Empress. The decorations were worn on specific ceremonial occasions with a court dress in the traditional Old Russian style. The dress was of white silk weighted by a gold and red velvet train complete with *kokoshnik* diadem of red velvet embroidered with gold. The ciphers were then pinned to the left shoulder on a St. Andrew's sash of pale blue moiré silk. Once married, the *demoiselles des Imperatrices* would renounce their positions as Maids of Honor, but would be allowed to keep their diamond decorations.

With special thanks to Ulla Tillander-Godenhielm for the above information.

Provenance:

Jointly presented by the Dowager Empress Maria Fedorovna and Empress Alexandra, wife of Emperor Nicholas II to a selected Maid of Honor.

Purchased from Marie E. Betteley, New York

Estimate: $25,000 - $35,000

IMPORTANT TSAR ALEXANDER I DIAMOND AND ENAMEL
IMPERIAL PRESENTATION BRACELET

36030

Important Tsar Alexander I Diamond and Enamel Imperial Presentation Bracelet

St. Petersburg, early 19th century, unmarked, possibly by the Théremin brothers

The center applied with crowned initial *A* for Alexander I Pavlovich, Emperor of Russia (r. 1801-1825), set with rose diamonds on an oval royal blue *guilloché* enameled plaque, surrounded by twelve graduated old mine-cut diamonds within an openwork diamond surround of scrolls set with old mine-cut diamonds framing two diamond clusters, each comprising a central old mine-cut diamond surrounded by nine old mine-cut diamonds, attached to a royal blue *guilloché* enamel and gold hinged bangle, diamond section may be detached to form a brooch-central enamel plaque with diamond surround-1 3/4 in. long; entire diamond section-2 1/4 in. wide. Total approximate weight of diamonds: 18.50 carats

Alexander I (1777-1825)

Russia's most enigmatic Tsar, Alexander reigned from 1801 to 1825. He was brought to power by a palace coup and reversed the reactionary course on which his murdered father, Paul I, had set Russia. The liberal first half of his reign came to an end when Napoleon invaded Russia in 1812. Alexander's defeat of the French marked one of the most glorious epochs of Russian history.

Set with the Tsar's crowned diamond initial, this bracelet of outstanding workmanship was presented by the Emperor at the turn of the 19th century. Although the recipient is as yet unknown (this may surface with archival research), bejeweled gifts bearing the cipher of the Sovereign were usually destined for members of the Russian or European nobility, people close to the Imperial family, and foreign court dignitaries. Although unmarked, the bracelet's crosshatched *guilloché* pattern, monogram design, and diamond settings are characteristics of the Russian workmanship of the Théremin brothers of St. Petersburg, court jewelers and members of the foreign masters guild who settled in Russia in 1793. For an Alexander I diamond ring of similar inspiration in the Hermitage Museum, see *Gold of the Tsars: 100 Masterpieces of the Hermitage St. Petersburg,* Stuttgart, 1995, p. 179. And for an Alexander I presentation box by Pierre Théremin, see Alexander von Solodkoff's *Russian Gold and Silverwork,* New York, fig. 194.

Few examples of Russian early 19th century Imperial jewelry ever appear on the market. No other comparable Alexander I bracelet seems to have surfaced at auction in the past 30 years.

Provenance:

Purchased from A la Vieille Russie

Estimate: $100,000 - $150,000

The Russo Collection is being sold without consignor reserves. All lots will open at 50% of the low estimate.

Session One, Auction #5003 | Thursday, April 24, 10:00 AM CT   35

36031

Pair of Imperial Russian Military Buttons Mounted as Cufflinks

The buttons circa 1900

Circular, each applied with a Russian Imperial eagle, the reverse reads *K. u. K Hof, Liferante* with double-headed eagle, each attached to a gold-plated link-diam. of button-approx 1 in.

Provenance:

Purchased from A la Vieille Russie

Estimate: $400 - $600

36032

Nicholas and Alexandra Silvered Metal Quatrefoil Brooch

Circa 1896

Inset with the portraits of the Imperial couple-1 ½ in. diam.

Estimate: $100 - $200

Rare Imperial Russian Gilt Brass Judge's Collar

19th century

Designed as a long chain of closely connected openwork oval links enhanced on each side with a Russian Imperial eagle, each attached to a Column of Justice motif inscribed in Russian *Justice* below a Romanov crown, suspending in the center a larger Imperial Russian double-headed eagle-4 in. long; the chain approx. 40 in. long. Sold together with a framed miniature of Tsar Nicholas II, both within a larger frame.

Provenance:

Purchased from Marie E. Betteley, New York

36034

Russian Imperial Silver Jeton Mounted as a Bookmark

Early 20th century

The shield-shaped silver badge of white enamel applied with the crowned Cyrillic initials *NA* for Nicholas Alexandrovich, Emperor of Russia (r. 1894-1917), the border decorated with Russian inscription *Okhtenskoe bratstvo* (Okhtenskii brotherhood) on blue enamel with date *1906*, attached to silver bookmark-3 in. long

Estimate: $1,000 - $2,000

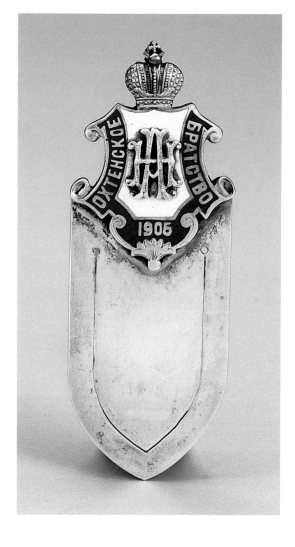

36035

Imperial Russian Tsar Alexander II Justice of the Peace Brass Badge

Dated 20 November 1864 in Cyrillic

Shaped oval, with crowned cipher of Alexander II, Emperor of Russia (r. 1855-1881) and central Russian Imperial double-headed eagle-3 3/8 in. long

Estimate: $300 - $400

Rare Russian Enameled Imperial Order of St. Anne

Late 19th century, unmarked

Second Class, designed as a red enameled Maltese cross, the arms
outlined in gold, the center inset with a circular medallion of white
enamel depicting the figure of Saint Anne, with mountains and trees
in colored enamel, on the reverse also enameled are the first letters
of the motto *AMANTIBUS, JUSTITIAM, PIETATEM, FIDEM* (To those
who love Justice, Piety, and Fidelity), set with pastes between the
arms and on the suspension ring-50 mm long; with diamond-set
suspension ring-2 3/4 in. long, attached to original red and yellow
moiré silk ribbon, in original oxblood leather-fitted box stamped *F.
Butz, St Petersburg*

Duke Charles Frederick of Schleswig-Holstein founded the order in
1735 in memory of his wife, Anna Petrovna, daughter of Peter the
Great. The Duke began to confer the order to Russians when his
son, the future Emperor Peter III, went to Russia in 1742. Later that
century, Tsar Paul I established the order as purely Russian. It was
awarded primarily for a long and distinguished career in the civil
service, the clergy, or the military. Badges of the Second Class were
worn on a sash suspended from the neck.

Provenance:

Purchased from Russian Arts Inc., New York

36037

Rare Imperial Russian Gold and Enameled Equestrian Award

Circa 1907

The shaped outline surmounted by a Romanov crown above a Russian Imperial Eagle within a horseshoe in gold, surrounded by the abbreviated Cyrillic inscription loosely translated as *Imperial Society of Encouragement for Equestrian Training.* The reverse inscribed *K.K. Smirnov* on a gold ribbon and dated February 14, 1907-45 mm long

Estimate: $1,000 - $2,000

36038

Imperial Russian Enameled Silver-Gilt Grand Duke Michael Commemorative Badge

By Eduard Johan Kortman, St. Petersburg, 1906

Designed as a Romanov crown adorned with the orange and black enamel ribbon of the Imperial Order of Saint George, with initial *M* on crossed miniature cannons of oxidized silver and the dates *1856-1906*, and Latin letter *L* for 50 years-2 in. long

Michael Nikolaevich (1832-1909)

Grand Duke Michael was born in Peterhof in 1832, the fourth son of Emperor Nicholas I. As Viceroy of the Caucasus and a general in the Crimean War, he proved a strong and passionate military leader. He conducted a typically lavish grand ducal lifestyle in his many palaces, in St. Petersburg, Tiflis, and in Mikhailovskoe on the Baltic. His summer residence on the estate of Borzhom, now a natural parkland in Georgia, was roughly the size of Holland.

Eduard Johan Kortman

Supplier to the Russian Imperial court, Kortman owned a gold and silver workshop since 1848. Located on Nevsky Prospect, no.34, his firm was renowned for enameled jetons, imperial badges and other fine gold objects. The jeweler received the Order of Saint Stanislaus, Third Class, and the Order of Saint Anna, Second Class, and also worked for the House of Fabergé.

Provenance:

Presented to Grand Duke Michael Nikolaevich (1832-1909) to commemorate the 50th Anniversary of his serving as Inspector General of the Artillery.

Purchased from A la Vieille Russie

Estimate: $1,000 - $1,500

36039

Russian Gold and Enameled Badge

Stamped 72 for 18k

Designed as a quatrefoil, the front centered by a crowned black enameled Imperial double-headed eagle, the raised border inscribed in Russian, *To the Esteemed Justice of the Peace, City of Odessa*, the reverse inscribed, *In token of gratitude, to Grigorii Salomonovich Gurovich, 1871* -1 3/4 in. long, in a new box

Exhibited:

New York, Metropolitan Museum, *Fabergé in America*, 1996, no. 34, illustrated.

Provenance:

Christie's, New York

Estimate: $2,000 - $3,000

36040

Imperial Russian Enameled University Badge

Circa 1900

Designed as a white enameled lozenge applied with a blue enameled cross, surmounted by the Russian Imperial Eagle in silver-65mm long including eagle. In original red presentation box.

Estimate: $500 - $700

The Russo Collection is being sold without consignor reserves. All lots will open at 50% of the low estimate.

Session One, Auction #5003 | Thursday, April 24, 10:00 AM CT   41

36041

Russian Imperial Presentation Brass Seal of the Great State Arms

19th century

Circular, the slip-on cover applied with the Russian Imperial double-headed eagle within a shield enclosed by the Imperial mantle, below the orb and Romanov crown, surrounded by an applied laurel and oak wreath, containing original wax Imperial seal, attached to a braid and tassel-11 1/2 in. diam.

Provenance:

Christie's, New York

Estimate: $3,000 - $5,000

36042

Imperial Russian Empress Catherine the Great Silver Table Medal

Later mounted on a silver box, the medallion depicting a bust of Catherine II Alexeevna, Empress of Russia (r. 1762-1796) facing right, wearing Imperial Romanov crown, with deep décolletage, after a portrait by *I. B. Gass* in Russian *KOP A. KLI* with inscription around edge, the reverse with scene of full-length goddess Ceres holding staff and wreath in landscape, with Cyrillic inscription *REWARD FOR GOOD DEEDS*- 65 mm. diam; the box American, 20th century, stamped sterling-3 5/8 x 3 x 3/4 in.

Estimate: $500 - $700

36043

Russian Imperial Table Medal

19th century

The obverse with full-length figure of Athena, goddess of wisdom and the arts, surrounded by the Cyrillic inscription *TO THE ONE WHO SUCCEEDS*, the reverse with a double headed eagle, in original fitted box-40 mm. diam.

Estimate: $300 - $400

36044

Imperial Russian Alexander I Karelian Birchwood Table Box

Circa 1812

Circular, the slip-on cover fitted with a gilded profile facing right of Emperor Alexander I of Russia (r. 1801-1825) after a portrait by Morel, bordered by the inscription *Alexander I Imp. Russorum* below a gold-mounted glass, the interior lined in tortoiseshell-3 1/4 in. diam.

Estimate: $1,500 - $2,000

36045

Imperial Russian Emperor Nicholas I Commemorative Silver Table Medallion

Stamped Moscow, 1908-17

The bust of the Tsar facing left wearing uniform and helmet of the Imperial Horse Guards after a portrait by P. Brusnitzin, 1859, surrounded by Russian inscription: *Nicholas I, Emperor and Autocrat of All the Russias, Born 23 June 1796, Died 18 February 1855,* within a raised laurel leaf border, framed with ring for outer suspension ring-4 in. diam., with leather backing

Nicholas I (1796-1855)

If his older brother, Tsar Alexander I, reflected the temperament of his grandmother, Catherine the Great, Nicholas I bore the imprint of their stern father, Paul I. Having acceded to the throne during the turmoil of the Decembrist Revolt of 1825, Nicholas ruled his empire with an iron hand. Born with a soldierly temperament, the Emperor was literally heartbroken by his beloved army's humiliating defeat in the Crimea, and he died in 1855, not long before the war's end.

Estimate: $400 - $600

36046

Russian Alexander II Silver Coronation Medal

1856

The obverse with profile of Alexander II, Tsar of Russia, with Cyrillic inscription *His Imperial Majesty Alexander II, Emperor Autocrat of All the Russias, Crowned in Moscow, 1856,* the reverse with Russian double-headed eagle below the words *God is With Us,* in a fitted red leather case-50 mm diam.

Alexander II (1818-1881)

Alexander II (r. 1855-1881) is fondly remembered by Russians as the "Tsar Liberator," whose most important achievement was to free his empire's serfs. Upon inheriting the throne from his stern father, Nicholas I, as Russia's autocratic edifice was severely shaken by defeat in the Crimean War, Alexander sought to revitalize his realm through his "Great Reforms." Ironically, on March 13, 1881, he was assassinated by terrorists on the very day he authorized a decree that would have put Russia on the path toward representative government.

Estimate: $500 - $700

36047

Imperial Russian Nicholas II Coronation Table Medal

1896

Commemorating the Imperial coronation of Tsar Nicholas II Alexandrovich (r. 1894-1917), the border inscribed in Russian *By the Grace of God Nicholas II Emperor and Autocrat of all the Russias,* the reverse with laurelleaf wreath and inscription *For Diligence,* attached to a red and white Saint Vladimir ribbon- 50 mm. diam.

Nicholas II (1868-1918)

A tragic figure, Nicholas suffered the fate of inheriting the Romanov Crown with neither the desire nor the temperament to be Emperor and Autocrat of the globe's most extensive empire. Russia's last Tsar reigned at a time of considerable stresses brought about by the modern age. A firm believer in his God-given prerogatives as an absolute monarch, Nicholas nevertheless proved capable of reform in times of crisis. However, his dynasty proved unable to weather its most severe test during the Great War.

Estimate: $200 - $300

The Russo Collection is being sold without consignor reserves. All lots will open at 50% of the low estimate.

Session One, Auction #5003 | Thursday, April 24, 10:00 AM CT   45

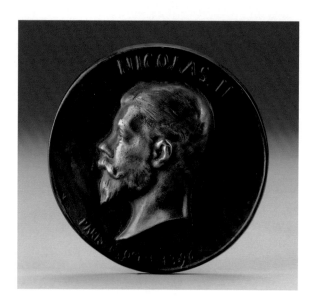

36048

French Nicholas II Bronze Table Medal

1896

Uniface, commemorating the Russian Emperor's visit to France, with the profile bust of Nicholas II, Tsar of Russia (1896-1917), inscribed *Nicolas* above and *Paris 6 Oct 1896*-4 in. diam.

Estimate: $100 - $150

36049

Russian Nicholas and Alexandra Bronze Table Medal

Circa 1896

Depicting the Imperial couple below a ribbon-tied Romanov eagle-4 in. diam.

Estimate: $100 - $200

36050

Imperial Russian Silver Table Medal of the Wedding of Nicholas and Alexandra

Circa 1894

One side depicting the profiles of Emperor Nicholas Alexandrovich and his betrothed Alexandra Fedorovna, each facing left, surrounded by Cyrillic inscription *In Memory of the Marriage of Emperor Nicholas II to Princess Alice of Hesse* and date *14 Nov 1894*, the reverse depicting the wedding of the Imperial couple in the Uspensky (Assumption) Cathedral of the Kremlin, unmarked- 55 mm. diam.

Provenance:
Purchased from Camden Market, London

Estimate: $800 - $1,200

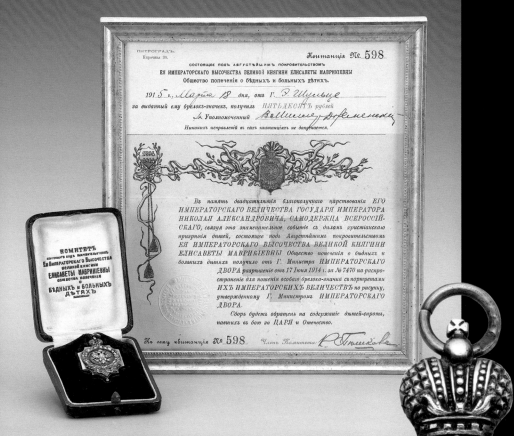

Russian Imperial Presentation Silver Badge of Honor in Original Fitted Box Commemorating the 20th Anniversary of the Nuptials of Emperor Nicholas II and Alexandra Fedorovna, with Award Document to F. Shulitse, Dated March 15, 1915

Stamped Moscow 1908-17

Designed as a silver shield-shaped locket surmounted by the Russian Imperial crown, the center with applied Romanov double-headed eagle within a wreath, opening to reveal the crowned ciphers of Nicholas and Alexandra above a photograph of the Imperial couple with the dates 1894 and 1914-2 in. high including suspension ring; award-8 1/4 x 7 1/2 in.

Provenance:
Purchased from Armoury of St. James, London

36052

Serbian Silver-gilt and Enamel Order of Saint Sava

Circa 1920

A Commander's neck badge, the silver-gilt ball-tipped cross decorated with blue-edged white enamel, small eagles in the angles between the arms, centering an oval portrait of the national Saint in red vestments, outer blue band is inscribed *By His Talents*- 87.7 x 49 mm including crown suspender, with original ribbon in case of issue

Estimate: $700 - $900

36053

Continental *Champlevé* Enameled Alexander II Brass Napkin Ring

Circa 1870

Cylindrical, overall enameled in cobalt blue decorated with foliate scrolls in brass within red enameled border, with the crowned initial *A* for Alexander II, Emperor of Russia (r. 1855-1881) in brass on bright yellow ground, within cartouche, the opposite side with vacant brass medallion on yellow ground-1 1/2 in. wide

Estimate: $200 - $300

RARE IMPERIAL RUSSIAN
FABERGÉ ALEXANDER III
25TH WEDDING ANNIVERSARY
PRESENTATION DESK CLOCK

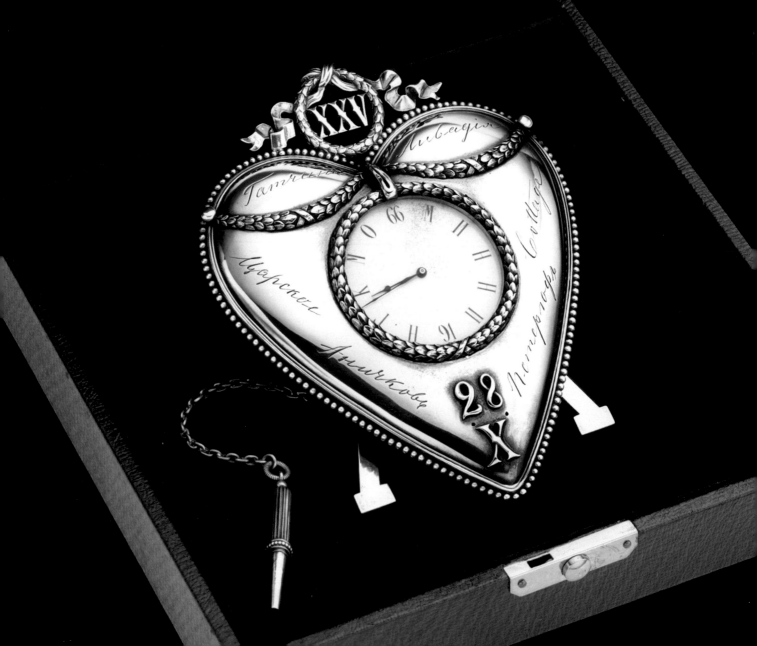

36054

Rare Imperial Russian Fabergé Alexander III 25th Wedding Anniversary Presentation Desk Clock

Workmaster Ivan Rappaport, St. Petersburg, circa 1891, signed IP, and Fabergé in Cyrillic

The heart-shaped silver clock engraved in Cyrillic script with the names of the Tsar's Imperial residences *Gatchina, Livadia, Tsarskoe (Selo), Anichkov, Peterhof,* and *Cottage*, the top applied with Roman numerals *XXV* within an openwork ribbon-tied laurelleaf wreath, the base, *28 X (October)*, enclosing a round white enamel dial with blue chapters, the years *(18)66* and *(18)91* as twelve o'clock and six o'clock respectively, the numerals one to five replaced by Cyrillic letters *M I N N I* spelling the Emperor's favorite name for the Empress, with the balance of the chapters represented by the first Cyrillic letter of each of their children's names: *N G K M O*, for Nicholas, George, Xenia, Michael, and Olga, within a raised laurel border, the silver strut forming the Tsar's initial *A*, the 8-day movement signed by Moser, with attached key on chain-5 1/2 in. high

Alexander III and Maria Fedorovna

The last Tsar to carry out his full reign, Alexander III ruled Russia from 1881 to 1894. Alexander acceded to the throne on March 14, 1881, a day after the assassination of his father, Emperor Alexander II, by a terrorist's bomb. Having inherited the Romanov crown in turbulent circumstances, Alexander III ruled his empire with an iron hand. Yet although he reversed some of his more liberal predecessor's reforms, he was not a blind reactionary. Alexander's thirteen-year reign witnessed the beginnings of industrialization, healthy state finances, and the start of the Trans-Siberian Railway. More important, the Emperor also restored his realm's stature as a great power after humiliating military and diplomatic defeats in the previous decades. Dubbed the "Tsar Peacemaker" (*Tsar mirotvorets*), Alexander was the only Romanov monarch for well over a century not to have seen his soldiers at war.

With a powerful six-foot physique, stern blue-gray eyes, and a full, black beard, Alexander III fully personified the mighty Russian autocracy. His strength was such that he entertained his guests by bending horseshoes and iron pokers. When at one state dinner the Austrian Ambassador hinted that his Emperor might mobilize two or three army corps on Russia's border to resolve a quarrel in the Balkans, Alexander calmly picked up a silver fork, tied it into a knot and placed it on the startled diplomat's plate, adding, "This is how I will deal with your corps." A man of simple tastes, the Tsar preferred the amusements of the hunt and the parlor to the more lavish pleasures of the St Petersburg court. Remarkably for a highborn Russian, Alexander was also utterly devoted to his wife, the Empress Maria Fedorovna.

Born Princess Dagmar of Denmark, the future Tsarina had been intended for Alexander's older brother, Grand Duke Nicholas Alexandrovich. However, the Tsarevich fell mortally ill, and on his deathbed is said to have placed his fiancée's hand in his brother's, commanding him to love her. Now the heir to the throne, Alexander III carried out the will, and the two were wed on November 9, 1866. By all accounts, the imperial couple enjoyed a harmonious and loving marriage. Maria presented her husband with five children, including the future Tsar Nicholas II.

The Empress was very careful not openly to interfere in politics. At the same time, she was the only person in Russia the Tsar allowed to influence his rule. It was partly at her urging that Alexander concluded the military alliance with the French Republic in 1894, a step that transformed European diplomacy.

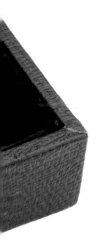

The Russo Collection is being sold without consignor reserves. All lots will open at 50% of the low estimate.

Session One, Auction #5003 | Thursday, April 24, 10:00 AM CT   51

Maria Fedorovna was much loved by her adopted subjects. The petite, dark-haired monarch was blessed with an out-going, gay temperament and easily made friends in St. Petersburg's notoriously venomous *haute monde*. Unlike her austere husband, Marie adored the glittering nightlife of the Imperial capital. By tradition, any ball she attended began with a lively mazurka, her favorite dance. Although she typically had a handsome young guards officer as her partner, her private life was irreproachable.

Despite his frugal ways, Alexander never stinted in presenting jewelry to his adored consort. Among the Empress's favorites was an imposing necklace with no less than nine strands of large pearls, all perfect in color and shape, held together with diamond fleur-de-lis clasps.

On the same silver wedding anniversary, the Imperial couple received from various relatives another silver clock by Fabergé that was massive, sculptural, and imposing. This understated Fabergé timepiece, privately commissioned by the Emperor for his wife symbolized their enduring love on a far more personal level.

Fabergé workmaster Julius Rappaport

Julius Rappaport (1851-1917) joined the House of Fabergé around 1890 and became Head Silver Workmaster of the St. Petersburg workshop. An excellent silversmith specializing in silver-mounted items in the classical style, the Imperial family entrusted Rappaport with the most important commissions. At the 1900 Paris World Exhibition, Rappaport won the Grand Prize for his famous miniature recreations of the Imperial regalia. Along with headworkmaster, Michael Perchin and his successor, Henrik Wigström, Rappaport was the only Fabergé workmaster in St. Petersburg to produce clocks for the Imperial Family.

Provenance:

Presented by Tsar Alexander III (r. 1881-1894) to his wife Maria Fedorovna on the occasion of their Silver Wedding Anniversary celebrated on October 28, 1891.

Purchased from A la Vieille Russie

Estimate: $300,000 - $500,000

36055

Imperial Russian Empress Maria Fedorovna Linen Handkerchief

Circa 1890

Of fine transparent white gauze folded in quarters, the corner embroidered with the crowned entwined initials *MF*, for Empress Maria Fedorovna (1847-1928) with lace border enhanced with embroidered floral sprays and garlands-7 x 6 3/4 folded, within later brown leather portfolio frame

Estimate: $500 - $800

36056

Russian Silk Pillow with Watercolor Portrait of a Young Woman

Square, according to back panel, embroidered by Empress Alexandra, wife of Tsar Nicholas II (r. 1894-1917), with a ribbon-tied foliate swag and crossed arrows above a circular watercolor portrait of a young woman signed *E B* and said to be by Grand Duchess Elizabeth (Ella) (1864-1918), Empress Alexandra's older sister, the back panel reads in Russian:

Embroidery

Her Imperial Majesty Empress

Alexandra Feodorovna

Aquarelle

Her Imperial Majesty

Grand Duchess Elizabeth Feodorovna

10 ½ in square, sold together with an accompanying envelope inscribed in Russian: *To my, kind, loving little niece Masha Trubetskaya*

On her birthday 3/16 July and name day 22 July/4 Aug.

From ? who loves her with all his heart

Teri Karl Guy (??)

Klamarg 22 July/4 Aug. 1957

During the summer of 1895, Empress Alexandra and her sister Grand Duchess Elizabeth spent time together at Peterhof, the Imperial residence in St. Petersburg, engaged in needlework and other artistic endeavors. The two were close as the Grand Duchess had played a major role in the betrothal of her younger sister to the Tsarevich and would give them presents every year on the anniversary of their wedding. After the tragic death of her husband, Grand Duke Serge Alexandrovich (b. 1857) by an assassin's bomb in 1905, Grand Duchess Elizabeth took the veil and devoted the rest of ther life to religious causes. On July 18th, 1918, the day after the assassination of the imperial family, she too was murdered by the Bolsheviks.

Provenance:

Purchased from A la Vieille Russie

Estimate: $1,200 - $1,500

The Russo Collection is being sold without consignor reserves. All lots will open at 50% of the low estimate.

36057

Russian Empress Alexandra Fedorovna Silk Garter

1918

The beige silk garter below a Romanov crown,
framed-approx 6 in. diam.

Provenance:

Said to have been found among the Tsarina's personal
effects in the bedrooms of the Tsar's palace in
Tsarskoe Selo in 1918, following the assassination of
the Russian Imperial family.

Purchased from A la Vieille Russie

Estimate: $2,000 - $3,000

36058

**Imperial Russian Tsar Nicholas II
Ceramic Coronation Beaker**

By Kuznetsov

This olive green ceramic beaker was
made by the M. S. Kuznetsov Factory
in Russia to commemorate the 1896
Coronation of the last Romanov
couple, Nicholas and Alexandra, the
front depicts the Moscow Coat of Arms
of Saint George slaying the Dragon,
centering an oak leaf garland with
Romanov crown, below the Cyrillic
inscription *Remember the Coronation*,
flanked by the crowned Cyrillic ciphers
of the Tsar Nicholas II and Tsarina
Alexandra Fedorovna, the beaker
which tapers slightly from bottom to
top measures- 4 5/8 in. high

Estimate: $700 - $900

36059

**Russian Emperor Nicholas II
"Khodinka" Cup**

1896

Ceramic on copper, called the *Khodinka* Cup, or Cup of Sorrows, made to commemorate the Russian Imperial Coronation of the last Romanov couple, Nicholas and Alexandra in 1896, the front depicts the crowned ciphers of Tsar Nicholas II and Tsarina Alexandra Fedorovna above the date *1896*, the reverse, the Russian Imperial double-headed eagle, decorated with a rust-colored and pale blue strapwork design below a gilt border-4 in. high

Four days after the Tsar's coronation, on May 18, 1896, close to half a million people gathered on the Khodynka Field northwest of Moscow, to celebrate the occasion and receive gifts, including this beaker, from the Imperial family. These were to be distributed the following morning. Early the next day, which was unseasonably hot, rumor spread about a shortage of souvenirs. The masses in a panic started to surge towards the distribution stalls causing widespread trampling and over a thousand deaths. Many saw the catastrophe at Khodynka Field as a bad omen for the Tsar's new reign.

Provenance:
Purchased from Hope & Glory, London

Estimate: $1,200 - $1,500

36060

**Imperial Russian Nicholas and Alexandra
Tin Coronation Beaker**

1896, St. Petersburg

The tin beaker decorated on one side with a Russian double-headed eagle above Cyrillic initials *NA* for Emperor Nicholas Alexandrovich (r. 1894-1917) and date *May 14, 1896*, the reverse with double portraits of the Tsar and Tsarina surrounded by Imperial ermine mantle below Romanov crown and orb and scepter, the Russian inscription *In Commemoration of the Imperial Coronation*-5 in. high

Provenance:
Purchased from Marie E. Betteley, New York

Estimate: $2,500 - $3,500

The Russo Collection is being sold without consignor reserves. All lots will open at 50% of the low estimate.

36061

A Pair of Cast Glass Busts of Nicholas and Alexandra

Circa 1900

Tsar Nicholas II (r.1896-1917) in military uniform on a raised plinth inscribed *Le Tsar Nicolas II, Bonbons John Tavernier,* Alexandra wearing a fur-trimmed décolletage, a pearl choker and a long pendant necklace above *La Tsarine*-13 in. high

Estimate: $1,000 - $1,500

36062

Small Nicholas and Alexandra Enameled Brass Souvenir Box

French, 1896

Commemorating the Tsar's visit to Paris in October, of brass surrounding clear beveled panels, the cover depicting in enamels the Imperial couple in separate oval frames centered by the initials *R.F.* for *Republique Française,* flanked by the *tricolore* above the date *1896*-2 x 3 x 2 5/8 in.

Estimate: $200 - $300

36063

Imperial Russian Photograph of Grand Duke Vladimir Alexandrovich in Original Frame

Depicting the Grand Duke (1847-1909) in full court uniform facing 3/4 to the dexter within an articulated oak frame, the corners decorated with scrolls, the top applied with Romanov crown with raised borders (three small pieces missing), wooden backing and strut- 10 5/8 x 9 1/8 in.

Vladimir was really a good connoisseur of everything concerning the arts. He was a good painter, and a patron of the ballet, particularly helpful to Diaghilev. He was highly intelligent, and better educated than most of his extended family, and was basically a very kind person. -Prince David Chavchavadze

The third son of Alexander II, Grand Duke Vladimir Alexandrovich was Commander of the Imperial Guard and President of the Academy of Fine Arts. He fulfilled this latter duty with zeal, and was particularly fond of the jeweler's art. He was an early fan of Fabergé, and helped his brother Tsar Alexander III commission the first Imperial Easter egg in 1885. In 1902, the Grand Duke held an exhibit of jewelry by the master at his palace, which included miniature replicas of the Romanov Crown Jewels.

Estimate: $2,000 - $3,000

36064

Original Presentation Photograph of Anastasie Mikhailovna, Grand Duchess of Russia (1860-1922)

The sepia toned photograph of the Grand Duchess signed *Anastasie* and dated 1891, in yellow velvet brass overlay frame, with Royal emblem- 13 x 9 ½ in.

Provenance:

Purchased from St. Petersburg Shop, Paris

Estimate: $2,000 - $3,000

The Russo Collection is being sold without consignor reserves. All lots will open at 50% of the low estimate.

36065

Original Photograph of Tsar Nicholas II

Handsome depiction of the Nicholas II, Tsar of Russia (r. 1894-1917) on horseback,
signed *Nicolai* in Cyrillic, and dated May 20, 1910- 14 x 15 in.

Estimate: $2,000 - $3,000

36066

**Original Invitation for a Reception to Honor
Grand Duke Alexander Nikolaevich, Future Tsar
Alexander II of Russia**

Printed invitation for a reception honoring the Grand
Duke eleven years prior to his reign, (r. 1885-1881), at
Guild Hall, on May 18, 1874, from the Honorable W.
Spencer Ponsonby, signed by Edward Hart; framed-
9 x 12 in.

Estimate: $100 - $150

36067

Imperial Russian Menu for the Wedding Banquet of Grand Duke Peter Nikolaevich and Princess Militsa of Montenegro

In Russian, dated July 26, 1889, Peterhof

Chromolithograph, depicting a double-headed eagle above Romanov Imperial crown amidst a bouquet of roses surmounting the oval shields of the respective royal families, the center with crowned initials of Grand Duke Peter Nikolaevich (1864-1931) and Princess Militsa (1866-1951) in Cyrillic with scenes of the two countries united-12 1/2 x 9 1/4 in. within a later frame

Since the days of Peter the Great, ties between the tiny Balkan Kingdom of Montenegro and Russia had been close. Nevertheless, Tsar Alexander III's efforts to secure Princess Militsa as the bride for Grand Duke Peter were not easy. While her father, King Nicholas of Montenegro, readily agreed to the match, the princess refused to leave without her sister Anastasia. The King threatened to ship her to St. Petersburg in chains to fulfil her dynastic obligations, but this drastic solution was averted when Alexander found another eligible cousin, the Duke of Leuchtenberg. While the duke was a "confirmed bachelor," the prospect of the immense dowry Alexander III promised to arrange led to a change of heart. Nicknamed "the black peril," the Montenegran sisters were prominent figures in *fin-de-siècle* St. Petersburg society. The duo also shared an avid interest in mysticism, and it was they who introduced Dr. Philippe and Rasputin to Empress Alexandra.

Provenance:
Purchased from Marie E. Betteley

Estimate: $1,500 - $2,000

36068

Imperial Russian Menu for the Wedding Banquet of Grand Duke Paul Alexandrovich and Princess Alexandra of Greece

Dated June 4, 1889, in French

Chromolithograph, depicting a Romanov Imperial crown above the arms of the Russian Empire and the Kingdom of Greece draped by the respective countries' flags with Cyrillic initials of Grand Duke Paul Alexandrovich and Alexandra, Princess of Greece (1870-1891), below a laurel branch, a scene of St. Petersburg above and scenes of Athens below, signed-12 1/2 x 8 1/4 in., in a later frame.

Paul Alexandrovich (1860-1919)

Only 21 years old, Alexandra, the Grand Duke's wife, died in childbirth only three years after their wedding. As a widower, the Grand Duke did not distinguish himself in the Imperial court. Close in age to Nicholas II, Paul Alexandrovich was a favorite uncle of the Tsar. Nicholas's fondness turned to disfavor for the Grand Duke however, when his mistress, Madame Olga Pistolkors, scandalized the court by sporting some diamonds that had once belonged to the late Empress Maria on her ample *décolletage* at a Winter Palace Ball. Forced into exile, the couple wed in Italy, but were eventually allowed to return to St. Petersburg. A little over a year after the Revolution, the Cheka executed the Grand Duke in the Saints Peter and Paul Fortress.

Provenance:
Purchased from Marie E. Betteley

Estimate: $1,500 - $2,000

36069

Imperial Russian Nicholas II Coronation Announcement

By Ivan Ropet, Moscow, 1896

Chromolithograph, an announcement of the Coronation of Emperor Nicholas II Alexandrovich and his consort Alexandra Fedorovna on May 14, 1896, in Old Church Slavonic script enclosed by colorful *Style Russe* strap work decoration, the top depicting a crowned Cyrillic N within a circular frame above the Order of Saint Andrew, flanked by two black Romanov double-headed eagles, the borders decorated with the Coats of Arms of various Russian towns-16 1/2 x 11 1/2 in., within a later frame

The Coronation of Tsar Nicholas II

The Coronation of Nicholas Alexandrovich was held on May 14th, 1896 in the Assumption Cathedral of the Moscow Kremlin. Costing over 100 million rubles, it was to be the final and most extravagant of Romanov coronations: kings, crown princes, presidents, and other heads of state from around the world traveled to the old capital to participate in the 20-day festivity. One journalist described the Kremlin's ambiance at twilight after the Imperial procession: "A magical fairytale began, a waking dream. People walked as if spellbound among glowing precious stones, the million lights of the city and the Kremlin, admiring the exotic sight".

Literature:

Elena Chernevich, *Russian Graphic Design, 1880-1917* (New York, 1990), p. 29.
For an example in the Hermitage Museum see, *Nicholas and Alexandra, the Last Imperial Family of Tsarist Russia,* London, 1998, p. 283.

Provenance:

Purchased from Marie E. Betteley, New York

Estimate: $5,000 - $7,000

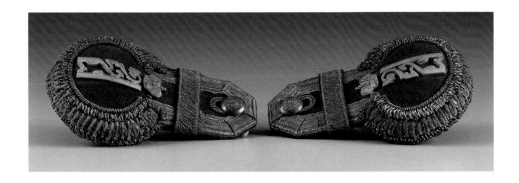

36070

Pair of Russian Regimental Epaulettes

Mid to late 19th century

Each applied with the Imperial crowned initial of Tsar Alexander II (r. 1855-1881) with gold braided trim on red felt-5 ¾ in.

Provenance:

Purchased from Russian Arts Ltd.

Estimate: $700 - $900

BRITISH &
PRUSSIAN

SESSION TWO | APRIL 24, 2008 | 12 PM CT

QUEEN ANNE
1702-1714
Anne was the last monarch of the House
of Stuart. She was succeeded by her
second cousin, George I, of the House of
Hanover, who was a descendant of the
Stuarts throguh his maternal grandmother,
Elizabeth, daughter of James I.

GEORGE I = Sophia Dorothea of
1714 - 1727   Brunswick and Celle

GEORGE II = Caroline of
1727-1760   Brandenburg-Anspach

Augusta of Saxe-Gotha = Frederick Lewis   William, Duke of Cumberland   Other children:
Altenburg   Prince of Wales   Anne   Mary
    Amelia   Louisa
    Caroline

Augusta   **GEORGE III** = Sophia Charlotte of   Other children:
    1760-1820   Mecklenburg-Strelitz   Edward   Louisa
    Elizabeth   Frederick William
    William   Caroline Matilda
    Henry

Caroline of Brunswick- = **GEORGE IV**   Frederick,   **WILLIAM IV**   Charlotte,   Other children: Mary
Wolfenbuttel   **1820-1830**   Duke of York   **1830-1837**   Princess Royal   Augusta   Sophia
    m. Adelaide of   Elizabeth   Octavius
    Saxe-Meiningen   Ernest Augustus   Alfred
    Adolphus   Amelia

Charlotte
m. Leopold of Saxe-Coburg,
later **LEOPOLD I** of Belgium   Victoria of = Edward, Duke of Kent
    Saxe-Coburg

Albert of Saxe- = **VICTORIA**
Coburg & Gotha   **1837-1901**

EDWARD VII = Alexandra   Princess Alice   Prince Alfred,   Princess Louise   Prince Leopold   Princess Beatrice
1901-1910   of Denmark   m. Grand Duke   Duke of Edinburgh
    Louis of Hesse   m. Maria Alexandrovna

    Princess Victoria   Princess Helena   Prince Arthur, = Louise Margarete
    m. **FREDERICK III**   m. Christian of   Duke of Connaught &   of Prussia
    of Prussia   Schleswig-Holstein   Strathearn

GEORGE V = Mary of Teck   Princess Margaret of
1910-1936   Connaught
    m. **GUSTAV VI** of Sweden

EDWARD VIII   **GEORGE VI** = Lady Elizabeth   Other children:
01.20.36 - 12.11.36   **1936-1952**   Bowes-Lyon   Mary   George
later, Duke of Windsor   Henry   John
m. Wallis Simpson

ELIZABETH II = Philip of Greece   Princess Margaret
1952 -   m. Antony, Earl of Snowdon

Charles, Prince of Wales = Lady Diana Spencer   Anne, Princess Royal   Andrew, Duke of York   Edward, Earl of Wessex
    m. Captain Mark Phillips   m. Sarah Ferguson   m. Sophie Rhys-Jones

Prince William of Wales   Prince Henry of Wales

The British and Prussian Royal Families

Colored names indicate those with items in the sale.

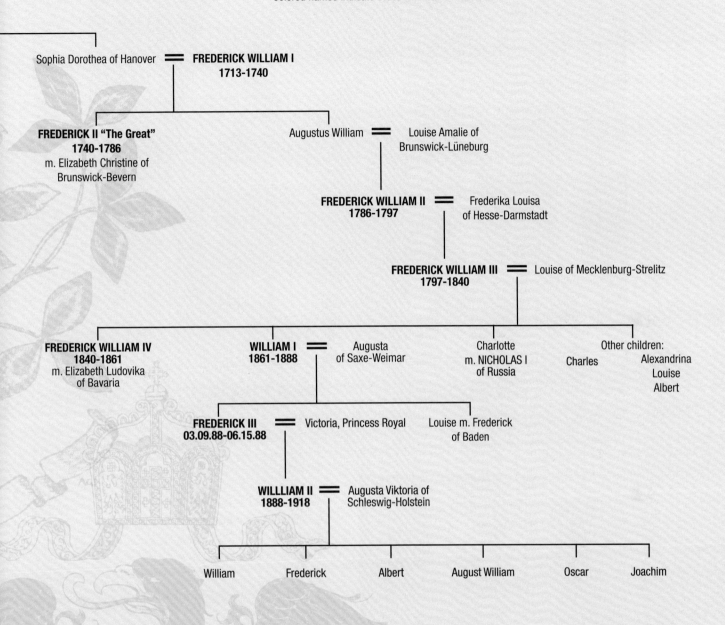

Sophia Dorothea of Hanover ══ **FREDERICK WILLIAM I**
1713-1740

FREDERICK II "The Great"
1740-1786
m. Elizabeth Christine of
Brunswick-Bevern

Augustus William ══ Louise Amalie of
Brunswick-Lüneburg

FREDERICK WILLIAM II ══ Frederika Louisa
1786-1797 of Hesse-Darmstadt

FREDERICK WILLIAM III ══ Louise of Mecklenburg-Strelitz
1797-1840

FREDERICK WILLIAM IV
1840-1861
m. Elizabeth Ludovika
of Bavaria

WILLIAM I ══ Augusta
1861-1888 of Saxe-Weimar

Charlotte
m. NICHOLAS I
of Russia

Other children:

Charles

Alexandrina
Louise
Albert

FREDERICK III ══ Victoria, Princess Royal
03.09.88-06.15.88

Louise m. Frederick
of Baden

WILLLIAM II ══ Augusta Viktoria of
1888-1918 Schleswig-Holstein

William   Frederick   Albert   August William   Oscar   Joachim

EMPEROR WILLIAM II

KING GEORGE V

QUEEN VICTORIA

36071

Pair of Miniature British Brass Parade Helmets on Stands

Early 20th century

One of the Royal Life Guards, the other of the 2nd or the Queen's Royal Regiment, applied with a horsehair plume, one encircled by the motto, *Honi Soit Qui Mal Y Pense* on a star, the other within an oak and laurel garland, each with neck straps on a columnar stand-the helmets: 8 in. high

Provenance:

Purchased from The Armoury of St. James, London

Estimate: $1,000 - $2,000

36072

Rare Georgian Brass Gorget for a Major

English, circa 1760

Of typical form, engraved with the crown initials *GR* for George III Rex (King) within laurel leaf bands-4 1/2 in.

Provenance:
Purchased from Forsyth's, Nashville, TN

Estimate: $1,000 - $2,000

36073

Gilt Metal Sword of the Bodyguard of King William IV (the Sailor King) of Great Britain and Ireland

Circa 1830

The scabbard of leather and gilt metal engraved with scrolls, one side applied with a brass plaque bearing the crowned inscription *Firmin & Sons Sword Cutters to His Majesty 153 Strand London*, the steel tapered blade similarly engraved and signed, with gilt metal hilt attached to pommel designed with tassel of silvered thread, one side embroidered with the initials *WR* for William IV, King of Great Britain (1830-37)- 38 1/2 in. long

Provenance:

Purchased from Forsyth's, Nashville, TN

Estimate: $3,000 - $4,000

The Russo Collection is being sold without consignor reserves. All lots will open at 50% of the low estimate.

Session Two, Auction #5003 | Thursday, April 24, 12:00 PM CT   67

36074

Pair of Regimental Epaulettes

19th century

Of typical form, the silvered tasseled epaulettes applied with sword and sheath below a royal crown-7 ½ in. long

Estimate: $100 - $200

36075

British Commemorative Regimental Drummer's Sash

1945

A ceremonial sash of intricate brocade on red leather backing, the front embroidered with British victories spanning 350 years, from *Namur 1695* to *Italy 1943-45*, and including *South Africa 1899*, *Salamanca (1812)*, *Loos (1915)*, *Gazala (1942)*, *Barrosa (1811)*, *Dettingen (1743)*, and *Talavera (1809)*, surmounted by the British Royal crown, a military star, and two drumsticks which fit into two pairs of loops sewn on the sides, with a tasseled base and red leather backing-61 in. long

Estimate: $800 - $1,200

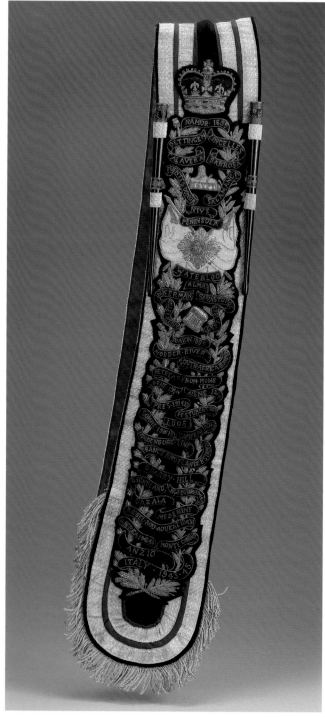

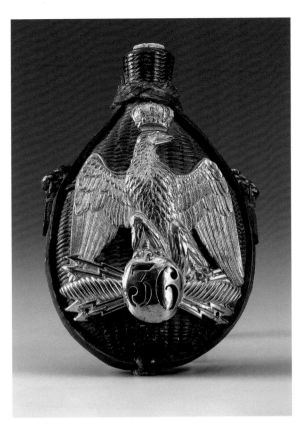

36076

Napoleonic Regimental Glass Campaign Flask

French, circa 1812

The glass flask with basket cover, the front applied with a large gilt metal Napoleonic crowned eagle perched on crossed arrows, above the gold and openwork *no. 36*, the sides mounted in brown leather, each side attached to a red, white, and blue cord, with cork-7 in. long x 5 in. wide

Napoleon (1769-1821)

Born Napoleone di Buonaparte in 1769 on France's recently acquired island of Corsica and trained at the Royal Military School in Paris, Napoleon adeptly translated a successful military career into political leadership during the turbulent years of the French Revolution. Crowning himself Emperor of France in 1804, the ambitious general launched a dramatic campaign that soon put large swaths of continental Europe under his scepter. It was only when he launched his ill-fated invasion of Russia in 1812 that his dreams of hegemony were dashed. Defeat at Waterloo on 18 June 1815 against an alliance led by Britain and Prussia confirmed the end of Napoleon's grand ambitions. Nevertheless, his many reforms in law and administration helped modernize much of Europe.

Provenance:

Purchased from Forsyth's, Nashville, TN

Estimate: $1,000 - $1,500

36077

Pair of Portuguese Epaulettes in Original Fitted Case

19th century

Royal Navy, each tasseled epaulette applied with a silver anchor and rope, one below the Royal crown of Portugal, in a tin carrying case lined in pink silk, the interior stamped *Bello, Lisboa*- epaulette-5 in. long

Estimate: $700 - $1,000

The Russo Collection is being sold without consignor reserves. All lots will open at 50% of the low estimate.

Session Two, Auction #5003 | Thursday, April 24, 12:00 PM CT   69

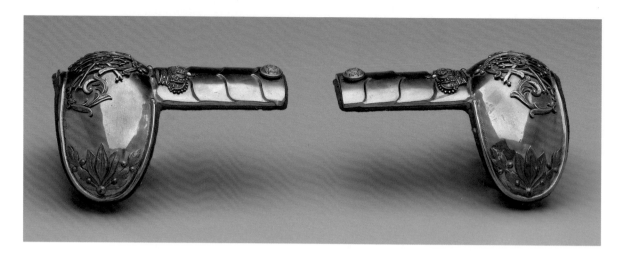

36078

Pair of Spanish Brass Epaulettes

Early 20th century

Each applied with a royal crown above entwined initials of Alfonso XIII, King of Spain (r. 1896-1931), the reverse stamped *Lucas Saenz, Madrid* on red felt backing-5 ½ in. long

Estimate: $800 - $1,000

36079

Austro-Hungarian Imperial Eagle Mounted on Wood

Circa 1890

4 ¼ in. diam.

Estimate: $100 - $150

36080

British Regimental Cartridge Case

1901-1914

A cartridge case of the Kings Own Yorkshire Light Infantry, the cover applied with a bugle and braid below the royal crown-6 in. wide

Provenance:

Purchased from Camden Passage, London

Estimate: $200 - $300

36081

British Army Cartridge Box

19th century

Royal Artillery, decorated with the British Royal Coat of Arms above a gilded cannon and Latin inscription *Quo fas, Et Gloria Ducunt* (Where Duty and Glory Lead)-6 ¾ in. wide

Provenance:

Purchased from Camden Passage, London

Estimate: $400 - $500

36083

British Leather Cartridge Box

19th century

With Royal emblem of two lions flanking a shield above inscription, on black leather-5 ½ in. wide

Provenance:

Purchased from Camden Passage, London

Estimate: $200 - $300

36082

George V Document Pouch

Circa 1915

Applied with the conjoined letters *GR* for *George, Rex*, King of Great Britain (r. 1910-1936) below the Royal crown and further decorated with a band of oak leaves, the leather and felt case with two compartments-5 ½ in. wide

Provenance:

Purchased from Camden Passage, London

Estimate: $300 - $500

36084

British George V Silver Cartridge Box

Birmingham, 1925

Applied with crowned initials, leather pouch missing-7 ¼ in. wide

Provenance:

Purchased from Camden Passage, London

Estimate: $150 - $200

The Russo Collection is being sold without consignor reserves. All lots will open at 50% of the low estimate.

Session Two, Auction #5003 | Thursday, April 24, 12:00 PM CT   71

36085

British George V Silver Cartridge Box

Circa 1915

Of typical form, set with the crowned brass initials *GRV* for George V, King of Great Britain (1910-1936), with leather interior compartment -6 ¾ in. wide

Provenance:

Purchased from Camden Passage, London

Estimate: $150 - $200

36086

British Royal Silver Plate Clothes Brush

Circa 1915

Rectangular, the surface applied with the crowned initials *PRDS*-7 ¼ in. wide

Provenance:

Purchased from Camden Passage, London

Estimate: $150 - $200

36087

British Oak Regimental Box

Circa 1940

Made from two George VI cartridge cases, opening from the center, each top cover centrally applied with the Royal star and crowned initials, mounted in oak-5 ¼ x 7 ¼ x 2 ¼ in.

Estimate: $150 - $200

36088

Austro-Hungarian Cartridge Box

Circa 1900

Of typical form and curving brass borders, the cover applied with the Imperial double-headed eagle of the Habsburg Empire, the red leather interior compartment fitted with detailed side panels depicting banners, swords, trumpets, and cannons-6 in. wide

Provenance:

Purchased from The Armoury of St. James, London

Estimate: $200 - $300

36089

Queen Victoria Enameled Gold and Gilt Metal Presentation Medal: Order of India

Circa 1880

Designed as a red enameled posey with green enamel leaves on gilt metal enclosing a high carat gold medallion bust of Queen Victoria facing left within a gold and blue enameled band inscribed *IMPERATRICIS AUSPICIIS* (Under the Protection of the Empress), surmounted by an openwork metal gilt crown, with large gold suspension ring-2 3/4 in. long including ring

Provenance:

Purchased from Kentshire Gallery, New York

Estimate: $2,500 - $3,500

36090

Rare Victorian Enamel, Diamond, and Gem-Set Baronet's Badge of Nova Scotia

English, circa 1874

Designed as a polished gold shield with red enamel lion rampant surrounded by small pearls, faceted emeralds, and sapphires below a red enamel and gold crown, within a blue enamel garter with motto *FAX MENTIS HONESTAE GLORIA* (Glory is the light of a noble mind), in gold framed by thirty-seven old mine-cut diamonds (averaging 2.5 mm), weighing approximately 1.85 carats total, the reverse engraved in Roman numerals for *March 30, 1874*, attached to an oval suspension ring-2 in. including ring, attached to an orange moiré silk ribbon, in original fitted blue leather box stamped *Spink & Son, Ltd, 5-7 King St. St. James, London SWI*

King James I of England granted the North American colony of New Scotland to Sir William Alexander in 1621 on the peninsula that today comprises the Canadian province of Nova Scotia. Ten years earlier, to support the settlement of Ireland, King James had instituted the hereditary Order of Baronets, a "new dignitie between Barons and Knights." On 28 May 1625, he created the Nova Scotia Baronets to support his overseas plantation. Baronets of Nova Scotia were asked to pay the Crown £2,000 (to support 6 colonists) and another £1,000 to Sir William. In 1629, King James authorized the badges, bearing the red lion rampant and suspended from an orange ribbon, for members of the order. No further Nova Scotia Baronets were created after the Act of Union of 1707, which joined Scotland with England in 1707. As a result, all present Nova Scotia Baronets are remnants of these ancient families.

Provenance:

Said to have been presented to Sir Alexander Jardine, 10th Baronet of Applegirth.

Purchased from The Armoury of St. James, London

Estimate: $10,000 - $15,000

The Russo Collection is being sold without consignor reserves. All lots will open at 50% of the low estimate.

Session Two, Auction #5003 | Thursday, April 24, 12:00 PM CT   75

Royal Prince of Wales Grenadier Guards Brass Badge

British, circa 1916

Mounted on a red velvet background and framed, the badge with voided center decorated with the cipher of King George V, the Order of the Garter and motto and surmounted by a King's crown, with original envelope inscribed by Queen Mary: *Grenadier badge worn on his steel helmet by the Prince of Wales from April 1916 till Octr 1917. He gave it to me. Mary R.*- 7 x 9 1/4 in.

Provenance:

Queen Mary
The Duke and Duchess of Windsor

Sotheby's, New York, *Property from the Collection of the Duke and Duchess of Windsor, 19th February 1998, lot 24*

36092

British Enameled Silver Medal

Circa 1959

Displaying enameled shield within green enameled laurel wreath, the reverse engraved *Alderman L.F. Davey, 1958-1959*, in case of issue with original ribbon

Estimate: $300 - $500

36093

Neck Badge of a Knight of the Sovereign Military Order of Malta

The white enamel arms with fleur-de-lis in between, below crown, attached to original black moiré silk ribbon, in original fitted case-82 mm long, including crown suspension

Estimate: $1,000 - $1,500

The Russo Collection is being sold without consignor reserves. All lots will open at 50% of the low estimate.

Session Two, Auction #5003 | Thursday, April 24, 12:00 PM CT   77

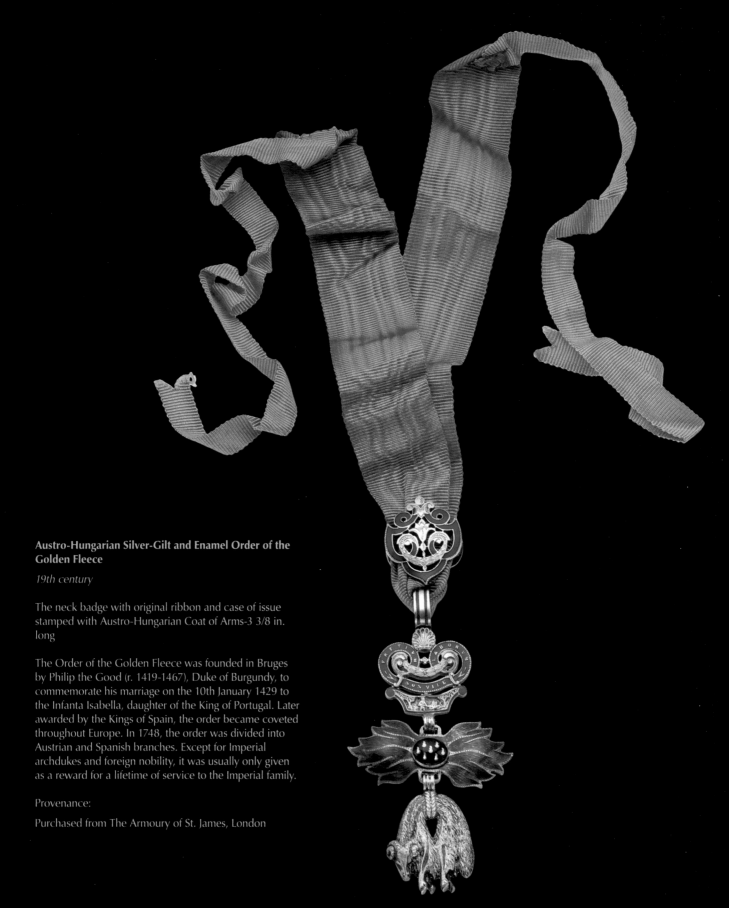

Austro-Hungarian Silver-Gilt and Enamel Order of the Golden Fleece

19th century

The neck badge with original ribbon and case of issue stamped with Austro-Hungarian Coat of Arms-3 3/8 in. long

The Order of the Golden Fleece was founded in Bruges by Philip the Good (r. 1419-1467), Duke of Burgundy, to commemorate his marriage on the 10th January 1429 to the Infanta Isabella, daughter of the King of Portugal. Later awarded by the Kings of Spain, the order became coveted throughout Europe. In 1748, the order was divided into Austrian and Spanish branches. Except for Imperial archdukes and foreign nobility, it was usually only given as a reward for a lifetime of service to the Imperial family.

Provenance:

Purchased from The Armoury of St. James, London

36095

Danish Gold and Enamel Order of the Dannebrog

Commander's neck Cross, by *Michelsen, Copenhagen*, 93mm x 48mm, surmounted by the crowned intials *C.IX.R.* for Christian IX, King of Denmark (r. 1863-1906), in case of issue stamped *Hof Ordens Juveleer A. Michelsen* and embossed with the eight-pointed star of the order

Christian IX (1818-1906)

Denmark's King from 1863 to 1906, shortly after he assumed the throne, his small kingdom was routed by the German states in 1864. In later years, he vainly resisted democracy until forced to yield to parliamentary government in 1901. Christian proved more adept at nuptial politics by marrying off his daughters Alexandra and Marie to the future King of England and Tsar of Russia, respectively.

Estimate: $1,200 - $1,500

36096

Imperial Austro-Hungarian Silver Military Inkwell

Circa 1890, stamped with Austrian hallmarks

On a rectangular silver plinth, an elaborate regimental helmet, the Imperial crest in front, oak leaf clusters on either side and on curved top, with swinging chin guard decorated with laurel leaves, forming the lid of inkwell in the center, which lifts on a hinge, further enhanced by applied axe and tied ropework on a blanket, entirely modeled in silver-9 1/4 x 5 1/2 x 5 in. high including helmet

Provenance:

Purchased from D. Podlewski, London

Estimate: $2,500 - $3,500

36097

Imperial Austro-Hungarian Franz Josef Gilt Bronze Household Chamberlain's Key

Circa 1870

Of elaborate design, the handle decorated with openwork foliate scrolls below a royal crown, attached to an embroidered crowned Habsburg double-headed eagle with tinsel, golden metallic threads and pailettes-5 5/8 in. long, in original brown leather fitted box

Provenance:

Probably presented by Franz Josef, Emperor of Austria (r. 1848-1916), King of Hungary (r. 1867-1916).

Purchased from The Armoury of St. James, London

Estimate: $800 - $1,200

36098

Damaged and Inscribed Silver Spoon with Royal Provenance in Fitted Case

Marked by William Eley I and William Fearn, London, 1799, marked on handle

A shell and scroll reeded tablespoon, twisted and broken in two parts, the handle engraved *tourné par le Prince Charles le 24 Janvier 1837*, the bowl engraved *Vermachtniss F. Kais. H. d. Grossf. Maria Nikol. Herzogin v. Leuchtenb. 1876*, in fitted case, the case - 4 3/4 in. long

As the younger brother of Empress Alexandra Fedorovna, Emperor Nicholas I's wife, Prince Charles was Grand Duchess Maria Nikolaevna's uncle. A general in the Prussian army, Prince Charles participated in King Wilhelm I's wars of German unification and amassed an enormous collection of weapons.

Provenance:

According to the inscriptions, this spoon was twisted by Charles-Frederick-Alexander, Prince of Prussia (1801-1883) in 1837 and was subsequently bequeathed to Grand Duchess Maria Nikolaevna, Duchess of Leuchtenberg, by the Prince in 1876.

Christie's, New York

Estimate: $1,200 - $1,500

36099

English Victorian Silver Royal Presentation Bachelor's Tea-Service

Marked Birmingham, with date letters N for 1862 (on cream jug) and V for 1870 (on teapot and cream jug) and maker's mark FE

Comprising a covered teapot, two-handled sugar-bowl, and cream-jug, each oval with partly gadrooned sides, the tea pot with gadrooned hinged cover and wooden finial, the front engraved *DR JAMES REID FROM VICTORIA R.I. XMAS 1888* , the reverse with crest below motto-the teapot-4 3/4 in high, in original red leather silk-lined fitted presentation case stamped *Elkington & Co.*

Provenance:

Given by Queen Victoria to Dr. James Reid, the Queen's surgeon

Purchased at Peter Kassai, New York

Estimate: $2,000 - $3,000

36100

Queen Victoria Commemorative Jubilee Pewter Mug

1887

A golden Jubilee mug, its base inset with transparent lithopane portrait of Queen Victoria above the inscription *1837 Jubilee 1887*-5 in. high

Provenance:

Purchased from Hope & Glory, London

Estimate: $100 - $200

The Russo Collection is being sold without consignor reserves. All lots will open at 50% of the low estimate.

Session Two, Auction #5003 | Thursday, April 24, 12:00 PM CT   81

36101

Royal Victoria and Albert Ivory-Handled Carving Set

English, probably commemorating the Royal wedding of 1840

A carving knife and fork of forged steel, each fitted with ivory handles, the fork carved with the head of Queen Victoria, the knife with that of the Prince Consort, Albert, each with crowned initial in black-the fork-11 in. long; the knife-15 in. long; in original fitted burgundy leather box

Provenance:

Purchased from The House of Hillman

Estimate: $1,500 - $1,800

36102

Victorian Silver-Plated Inkwell Commemorating Queen Victoria's Diamond Jubilee

English, circa 1897

In the form of the bust of Queen Victoria, wearing court regalia, the reverse inscribed *Victoria Regina, 50 Years, 1897*, the crown on her head lifting to reveal inkwell, on a square grooved base-7 1/4 in high

Provenance:

Purchased from Morning Glory, New York

Estimate: $800 - $1,200

36103

Small English Commemorative Silver Bust of King Edward VIII

Stamped Birmingham, 1936

Depicting Edward VIII, King of England and Emperor of India (r. 1936) facing right at 3/4 angle wearing military uniform, on a square plinth, also stamped *Made in England, copyright*-4 3/8 in. high

Estimate: $1,500 - $2,000

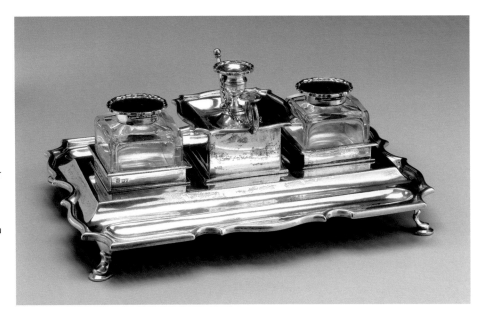

36104

British Silver Presentation Double Inkwell

1910

The rectangular shaped tray with two pen trays, mounted with two silver capped square bottles flanking a silver candle holder and miniature snifter, the front inscribed in part *Dr. T. Ross Macdonald, H.R. H. The Princess of Connaught* and dated *August 1910*, on curved feet-12 in. wide

Estimate: $2,500 - $3,500

36105

British Pewter Teapot Commemorating the Baptism of Edward VII

1841

Of bulbous form, on foliate capped legs, the slightly domed cover applied with a floral finial below which is engraved on scrolling ribbons *Born November 9th 1841-Bapd January 25th 1841*, with a curved spout and foliate-capped scroll handle -4 ½ in high

Provenance:

Purchased from Forsyth's, Nashville, TN

Estimate: $300 - $500

36106

British Edward VII Gilt Silver Coronation Spoon in Fitted Case

1902

A replica of the Coronation anointing spoon of Edward VII, the engraved bowl with central spine, with detailed tapering handle, in original leather box, the cover stamped *Edward VII, 26th June 1902*, the inside cover stamped *Reid & Sons, Goldsmiths & Jewellers to the Queen and Prince of Wales, Newcastle Upon the Tyne*-length of spoon-4 5/8 in.

On the coronation date of June 26, 1902, Edward VII was hospitalized for an emergency appendectomy. The coronation was postponed until August 9, 1902.

Estimate: $150 - $250

The Russo Collection is being sold without consignor reserves. All lots will open at 50% of the low estimate.

Session Two, Auction #5003 | Thursday, April 24, 12:00 PM CT   83

36107

British Queen Alexandra Enameled Silver-Gilt Pill Box

London, 1923

Of cornflower blue enamel, the center set with initials *AA* at cross angles for Alexandra, Queen Consort of Great Britain (1844-1925) below the British Royal crown-1 1/8 in. diam.

Estimate: $200 - $300

36108

British Queen Victoria Jubilee Silver Cigarette Box

by Hunt and Roshell, London, 1887

With patterned sides, the cover inset with a coin of the Sovereign dated 1888, the interior divided into two compartments-3 x 4 ¼ x 1 ½ in.

Estimate: $250 - $350

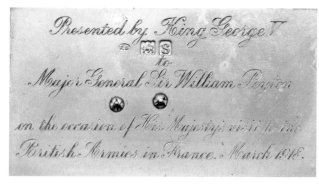

36109

English George V Silver and Enameled Royal Presentation Cigarette Case

Marked London, 1918, maker's mark F B

Rectangular with rounded corners, of vertical reeded design, with tinder cord compartment, match compartment and strike, the hinged cover applied with blue enameled *GRV* for George V Rex (King) of Great Britain (r. 1910-1936) below a gold and red enameled British Royal crown, the gilt interior inscribed *Presented by King George V to Major General Sir William Peyton on the Occasion of his Majesty's visit to the British Armies in France March 1918*-3 3/4 x 2 3/8 in. Together with description of General Sir William Eliot Peyton's military career

Provenance:

Purchased from The Armoury of St. James, London

Estimate: $1,200 - $1,500

Victorian Silver-gilt Presentation Snuffbox

Marked William Summers, London, 1868 WS N

Rectangular, of shaped outline, applied with a star of the order of the Queen's Own Light Infantry Militia below Royal British crown, in retailer's box with silver plaque engraved with dedication inscription (by Prince Arthur of Britain)

Queen Victoria's favorite son, Prince Arthur William Patrick of Saxe-Coburg-Gotha (1850-1942) was created Duke of Connaught and Strathearn in 1874. He had a distinguished military career, rising to Field Marshal in 1902, and served as Governor-General of Canada from 1911 to 1916.

Provenance:

Presented by Prince Arthur of Great Britain to the officers of the Queen's Own Light Infantry Militia, 1869.

Purchased at Asprey & Garrard's, London

36111

English Edward VII Silver and Enamel Royal Presentation Cigarette Case and Matching Vesta Case

Marked London 1901, maker's mark S & A

Each rectangular case of polished silver with rounded corners, the covers depicting a portrait of Edward VII, King of Great Britain (r. 1901-1910) facing left in full military uniform with decorations in *grisaille* enamel, on a blue *guilloché* background framed by the Royal garter and motto below the red enamel Royal crown, the background decorated with white *guilloché* enamel in a sunburst pattern-3 1/4 x 2 1/2; vesta case of similar design-2 x 1 3/4 in., the latter with suspension ring

Provenance:

Presented by King Edward VII (r. 1901-1911)

Purchased from Sheldon Shapiro, London

Estimate: $5,000 - $7,000

36112

Italian Royal Enamel *Carnet de Bal*

1913

The cover enameled with the crowned initials of Victor Emanuel III, King of Italy (r. 1900-1946), within floral garlands on a white *guilloché* enamel ground, fitted with a pencil and small note pad, the cover entitled *Ballo a Corte, 20 Gennaio 1913*-2 3/8 in. long

Estimate: $200 - $300

36113

Royal Presentation Silver Cigarette Case Given by King Ferdinand of Bulgaria

Circa 1910, 900 silver, inscribed 787435 with additional hallmark

The polished silver case applied with gold monogram forming a stylized Cyrillic *F*, for King Ferdinand I of Bulgaria (r. 1908-1918), accented with rose diamonds, below the Bulgarian Royal crown, the match compartment fitted with exterior match strike, attached to a silver ring and tinder cord displaying the Bulgarian national colors of red, green, and white-3 3/4 x 2 5/8 in.

Ferdinand Karl Leopold Maria of Saxe-Coburg-Gotha (1861-1948) was elected prince of the autonomous Ottoman principality of Bulgaria in 1887. Benefiting from one of the many Balkan crises of the time, he proclaimed full independence for Bulgaria in 1908, assuming the title of King, or Tsar. King Ferdinand sided with Germany and Austria-Hungary during the First World War and was forced to abdicate in favor of his son, Boris III, upon his Kingdom's military defeat in 1918. He subsequently lived in Coburg.

Provenance:

King Ferdinand of Bulgaria is said to have presented this case to King Farouk of Egypt

Purchased from Sheldon Shapiro, London

Estimate: $2,500 - $3,500

36114

French Emperor Napoleon III Gold and Diamond Presentation Snuffbox

Retailed by Froment-Meurice, Paris, circa 1855, maker's mark ?LB

Rectangular, the hinged cover decorated with scrolls on a matted ground, the center with initial *N* for Napoleon III, Emperor of France (r. 1852-1870) set with rose and old mine-cut diamonds below an Imperial diamond-set crown on an oval royal blue *guilloché* enamel plaque-3 1/2 x 2 1/4, in original red leather fitted case with crowned *N*

Napoleon III (1808-1873)

The nephew of his illustrious namesake, Napoleon III came to power through the ballot box when elected president of France after King Louis-Philippe was toppled from the throne by the 1848 Revolution. Constitutionally barred from a second term, he seized power in a coup d'état in 1852 and proclaimed himself Emperor. At home Napoleon III's rule improved the lives of the poor and saw Paris modernized under Baron Hausmann, but his adventurous foreign policy led to a disastrous war with Prussia in 1871, which cost him his crown.

Provenance:

Lady Keith Nancy

Christie's, New York

Estimate: $6,000 - $8,000

36115

French Napoleonic Silver Portrait Miniature Box

Circa 1880, with French hallmark on base

Oval, inset with individual portrait miniatures of Emperor Napoleon I of France (r. 1804-1814), his wife Empress Marie Louise (1791-1847), and their son, Napoleon II, the King of Rome (1811-1832), enclosed by a *repoussé* ribbon-tied garland surmounted by a crown, the border set with colored glass cabochons, with engraved sides and a gilt interior-3 5/8 in. wide; 1 1/4 in. high

Provenance:

Purchased from Lombard Antiquarian Maps & Prints

Estimate: $1,000 - $1,200

The Russo Collection is being sold without consignor reserves. All lots will open at 50% of the low estimate.

Session Two, Auction #5003 | Thursday, April 24, 12:00 PM CT   89

36116

Kaiser Wilhelm II Rose Gold Royal Presentation Cigarette Case

Circa 1895

The sleek square case of polished rose gold with rounded corners, overall decorated with a pebbled design, the upper left corner inset with diamond initial *W* for Wilhelm (William) II, Emperor of Germany, King of Prussia (r. 1888-1918) below a sapphire and diamond-set Imperial crown, fitted with cabochon sapphire pushpiece, the interior stamped *JOHN WAGNER & SOHN 585*, the inscription reads *To General F(?) Marshall from His Majesty, the Emperor of Germany, August 1895*-3 3/4 x 3 1/4 in.

William II (Kaiser) (1859-1941)

Emperor of Germany and King of Prussia from 1888 through 1918, William eschewed the careful diplomacy that had taken his realm to prominence in European affairs under the "Iron Chancellor" Prince Otto von Bismarck. While William did not seek war, his aggressive policies helped launch the calamitous Great War, which ultimately consumed four Imperial dynasties, including his own.

Provenance:

Given by Kaiser Fredrick Wilhelm Viktor Albert of Hohenzollern to Lieutenant General Marshall in 1895.

Purchased from Sheldon Shapiro, London

Estimate: $5,000 - $7,000

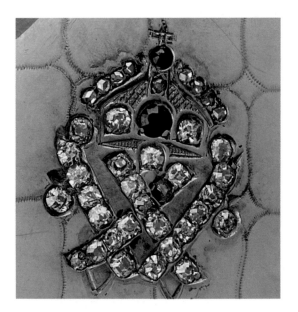

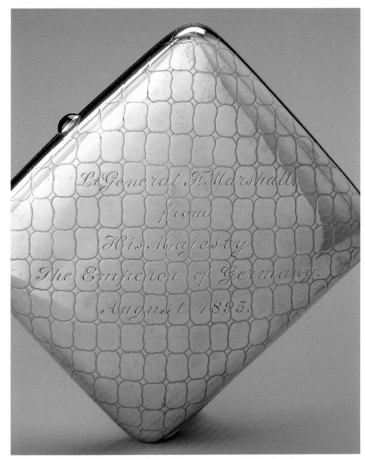

36117

Royal Swedish King Gustav VI Karelian Birchwood Cigar Box

Mid 20th century

Rectangular, of oval section, the hinged cover applied with the silver entwined initials *GA* for Gustaf VI Adolf, King of Sweden (r. 1950-1973) below Swedish Royal crown-5 7/8 x 3 7/8 x 1 in

Gustav VI Adolf (1882-1973)

King Gustav VI reigned over Sweden from 1950 to 1973. During his years as Crown Prince, Gustav combined a traditional military career with a less conventional in archeology. He participated in a number of digs in Asia and Europe, and was regarded an authority on Chinese pottery. Shortly before his death, the Riksdag (legislature) stripped the Swedish monarchy of its remaining constitutional powers upon the accession of his heir, King Carl XVI, in 1973.

Estimate: $800 - $1,200

36118

Royal Presentation Box Made for the Wedding of Princess Victoria and Crown Prince Frederick William

German or English, 1858

Oval, of brown tooled leather displaying the Coats of Arms of the German and British royal families below the German Imperial crown accented in gilt, on a hinge, opening to reveal a silver table medallion with similar decoration, the reverse with a bust of Queen Victoria within a beaded border, inset into a removable navy blue oval silk frame attached to a strut-box-4 3/8 in. wide; medallion-2 1/4 in. diam.

Emperor Friedrick III (b. 1831, r. 1888) of Germany married Victoria Adelaide Mary Louisa (1840-1901), Princess Royal of Great Britain and eldest daughter of Queen Victoria, at the Chapel Royal, St. James' Palace on January 25, 1858. The Emperor died of cancer after reigning only ninety-nine days and was succeeded by his son, William II.

Provenance:

Purchased from The Armoury of St. James, London

Estimate: $800 - $1,200

The Russo Collection is being sold without consignor reserves. All lots will open at 50% of the low estimate.

Session Two, Auction #5003 | Thursday, April 24, 12:00 PM CT   91

36119

Imperial Prussian Silver Seal Box

Late 19th century

Circular, the slip-on cover decorated with the Prussian Eagle clutching orb and scepter, within laurel border containing original wax imperial seal, and tasseled braided cords-6 in. diam.

Provenance:
Purchased from The Armoury of St. James, London

Estimate: $2,500 - $3,500

36120

Royal Gold and Enameled Wilhelm II Presentation Triple Pencil

Unmarked, circa 1890

The gold pencil surmounted by a royal crown, each textured tubular segment edged with red, blue, or black enamel in the color of the lead it propels, the center applied with Kaiser Wilhelm's enameled cipher-4 3/8 in. long

Provenance:
Sotheby's, London

Estimate: $2,500 - $3,500

36121

Portrait Miniature of George III

Circa 1800

On ivory, George III, King of Great Britain and Ireland (r. 1750-1820), grandfather of Queen Victoria, facing right, wearing a wig and red military uniform, within a paste border, together with a display box-3 ¼ in. including suspension ring

George III (1738-1820)

George III was both the sovereign of Great Britain and Ireland as well as Hanover. His sixty-year reign witnessed two major victorious wars with England's traditional enemy, France, but also the loss of most of its American colonies. In addition to these geopolitical challenges, during the latter decades of his reign George increasingly struggled with the more personal demons of madness probably induced by porphyria. Parliament declared the Prince of Wales regent in 1811.

Estimate: $2,000 - $3,000

36122

Royal Portrait Miniature of Young Queen Victoria

Circa 1840

Of *verre églomisé*, facing the viewer wearing a gold crown and necklace above an ermine-trimmed robe, on a gold pane, within an oval gilded frame, in original leather case-1 7/8 in. long

Estimate: $500 - $700

The Russo Collection is being sold without consignor reserves. All lots will open at 50% of the low estimate.

Session Two, Auction #5003 | Thursday, April 24, 12:00 PM CT   93

36123

Royal Portrait of Edward VII as Prince of Wales

French, circa 1875

Hand-painted photograph depicting the Prince wearing a uniform and medals, mounted on ceramic plaque, the reverse signed *Procédé Deroche, 29 Blvd. des Capucines, Paris, 1875*, with a gilt bronze frame surmounted by applied Prince of Wales Feathers, ribbons, and foliate garlands in gilt bronze, the interior of frame with painted stylized scrolls and foliage on pale gold background- 9 x 6 in.

Estimate: $1,200 - $1,500

36124

Royal Portrait of Edward VII as Prince of Wales

Circa 1900

Pastel, showing the Monarch in red full-dress uniform adorned with numerous badges and stars with gray overcoat, within a gilt bronze frame decorated with foliate scrolls surmounted by a crown.

Estimate: $2,000 - $3,000

36125

Pair of Portrait Miniatures of George V and Queen Mary

Circa 1915

Printed on paper, the monarch wearing full court uniform, the Queen with a diamond tiara, multiple strands of pearls and a pink gown, each within an oval brass frame, with individual miniature brass easels-miniature-2 ½ in. long; easel-5 ¼ in. long

Estimate: $400 - $600

36126

King Edward VII Portrait Miniature

Probably French, circa 1910

The oval miniature painted on ivory depicting Edward VII, King of Great Britain and Emperor of India (r. 1901-1910) in full court regalia wearing ermine mantle and medals, signed *Derval,* mounted on a green velvet backing accented with a paste border, within a gilt bronze rectangular frame with stiff-leaf border, surmounted by a heraldic crest flanked by laurel leaves-miniature-3 1/4 in. long; frame-10 x 6 1/2 in.

Provenance:

Purchased from Federico Carrera

Estimate: $1,200 - $1,500

The Russo Collection is being sold without consignor reserves. All lots will open at 50% of the low estimate.

Session Two, Auction #5003 | Thursday, April 24, 12:00 PM CT   95

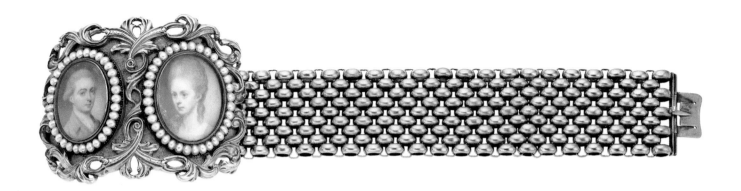

36127

Rare Regency 18 Karat Gold Bracelet Belonging to the Earl and Countess Grosvenor

English, circa 1820

The front of the cartouche curved outline with entwined raised foliate design in polished gold, applied with a pair of *grisailles* miniatures on copper, said to be of the Grosvenors, each within seed pearl frames, the reverse containing plaited locks of hair and respective initials *RG* and *TG* below glass, attached to a wide gold link mesh bracelet-the front- 2 3/4 in; the bracelet-5 1/4 x 1 in.

Having invested during the early 18th century in property in Mayfair, then an area of dubious repute on London's outskirts, the Grosvenors are one of Britain's wealthiest families. In 1874 Queen Victoria promoted Hugh Lupus Grosvenor from Marques to Duke of Westminster, creating the last non-royal duchy in England. As a result, the Duke of Westminster holds the paradoxical distinctions of being both the richest hereditary peer and last in precedence among Great Britain's ducal houses.

Provenance:

Purchased from Sheldon Shapiro, London

Estimate: $6,000 - $8,000

36128

Victorian Portrait Miniature of a Viscount Mounted on a Gold Bracelet

Miniature attributed to Sir William John Neweighton, circa 1840

The center designed as an oval gold locket, the hinged cover engraved with scrolls applied with small turquoise cabochons forming entwined initials below a seven-pointed coronet, with two serpent heads set with turquoises and garnet eyes encircling the top and bottom, the lid opening to reveal a signed portrait miniature on copper of a young Viscount, head and shoulders to the dexter with dark brown hair and side-whiskers, wearing a dark cravat, white waistcoat and black jacket, the miniature and locket attached to a paneled curved bracelet enhanced with engraved patterns and scrolls along the border-miniature including case and serpents-2 1/4 in. long

Provenance:

Purchased from Sheldon Shapiro, London

Estimate: $8,000 - $12,000

A 19.5% Buyer's Premium applies to all lots.
Visit HA.com/FineArt to view scalable images and bid online.

36129

English Gold Presentation Bracelet with Miniature

Circa 1850, unmarked

The center designed as an oval gold locket, the cover decorated with entwined double cipher in black enamel below a coronet of a Countess or Baroness, the cover opening to reveal painted miniature of a young boy said to be of Edward VII, Prince of Wales (1841-1910) possibly by Franz Xaver Winterhalter (1806-1873), within a frame of entwined gold ribbons, attached to a thick oval link bracelet in 18k gold-front section-3 in. long; the bracelet-7 1/4 in. long

Provenance:

Purchased from Sheldon Shapiro, London

Estimate: $8,000 - $12,000

36130

Gem-Set Queen Alexandra Royal Presentation Brooch

Early 20th century

Designed as two entwined initials *AA* for Queen Alexandra (1844-1925), one set with seed pearls, the other with antique-cut faceted diamonds averaging approximately 2 mm, surmounted by a blue enamel ribbon and rose diamond and enamel crown-1 in. wide

Provenance:

Purchased from The Armoury of St. James, London

Estimate: $2,500 - $3,500

36131

George V Gold and Gem-Set Royal Presentation Hunting Scarf Pin

English, maker's mark C.P.

A straight pin of 15k gold, the center applied with a circular gold disc inset with the initials *G.R. V* for George V Rex (King), gem-set with small rubies, sapphires, and diamonds below a crown set with rose diamonds-diam. of plaque-7/8 in. long, the pin-2 in. long

Provenance:

Purchased from The Armoury of St. James, London

Estimate: $800 - $1,200

36132

King George V and Queen Mary Enamel, Diamond, and Gold Royal Presentation Cipher

English, circa 1915

Circular, of openwork design, the center with diamond-set entwined initials *GM* for George V, King of Great Britain (1910-1936) and his consort, Queen Mary (1867-1953), mounted in platinum-topped gold, surmounted by a red enameled crown with a blue enameled ribbon inscribed *HONI SOIT QUI MAL Y PENSE* (shame to him who thinks evil of it), forming the Most Noble Order of the Garter, Britain's highest order of Chivalry-1 1/4 in. long including crown

Literature:

Philip Ziegler, *Mountbatten, The Official Biography* (London: Collins, 1985) pp. 34, 101.

Provenance:

Presented by King George V to Princess Alice of Greece (1885-1969). Eldest Child of Prince Louis of Battenburg (cr. Marques of Milford Haven 1917) and Princess Victoria of Hesse-Darmstadt (1863-1950); a great granddaughter of Queen Victoria; elder sister of Louis, Viscount Mountbatten of Burma; mother of the Duke of Edinburgh; and mother-in-law to the Queen Elizabeth of Great Britain.

Purchased from The Armoury of St. James, London

Estimate: $3,000 - $5,000

36133

Sapphire, Diamond, and Enamel George V Royal Presentation Brooch

English, circa 1913

Circular, of openwork cagework design, the center set with diamond entwined initials *GM* below the Royal crown of the House of Windsor, within a white enameled frame set with six light blue sapphire collets, each flanked by rose diamonds, in original box stamped *Collingwood & Co. To the Royal Family, 46 Conduit Street, London*, the front embossed with crowned initials-1 1/4 in. diam.

Provenance:

Given by King George V (r. 1910-1936) and Queen Mary.

Purchased from Sheldon Shapiro, London

Estimate: $5,000 - $7,000

The Russo Collection is being sold without consignor reserves. All lots will open at 50% of the low estimate.

Session Two, Auction #5003 | Thursday, April 24, 12:00 PM CT   101

King George V Portrait Miniature Mounted as a Diamond Brooch

English, circa 1915

Depicting the Monarch in full dress uniform facing forward surrounded by thirty-four circular-cut diamonds weighing approximately 3.04 carats total, mounted in platinum, the reverse set with an oval engine-turned gold plaque applied with the entwined rose gold initials *GR V* for King George V, below a red enamel and gold crown-1 3/8 in. long, including frame

George V (1865-1936)

A popular monarch, King George V was a reassuring presence during the First World War and the difficult decades that followed. He had begun his career in the Royal Navy, but when his elder brother unexpectedly died in 1892, George began a more rigorous education to prepare for the crown. He took as his wife his late brother's fiancée, Princess Mary of Teck.

Provenance:

Worn by a Court attendant.

Purchased from A la Vieille Russie

36135

Queen Alexandra Gold Lady-in-Waiting Brooch

Circa 1905

Oval, of openwork design, forming the entwined scrolling initials of Queen Alexandra (1844-1925), within a strapwork frame below a Royal crown-1 1/4 in. wide, in original blue leather Royal presentation fitted box stamped *Jewellers To the Royal Family, 46, Conduit Street, London*

Estimate: $1,200 - $1,500

36136

Queen Alexandra Diamond and Enamel Royal Presentation Stickpin

Circa 1905

Oval, decorated with turquoise *guilloché* enamel set with the rose diamond crowned initials *AA* for Queen Alexandra (1844-1925), within a rose-cut diamond border, enhanced with four pearls averaging 2.8 mm, mounted in gold-2 7/8 in. long, in original red leather fitted case stamped *Ryan & Co. Jewellers Dublin*

Provenance:

Given by Queen Alexandra

Purchased from S.J. Shrubsole, New York

Estimate: $2,500 - $3,500

36137

Oval Queen Alexandra Enameled Gold and Diamond Royal Presentation Brooch

English, circa 1905

Of violet *guilloché* enamel, the center set with entwined rose diamond initials *AA* at cross angles for Queen Alexandra (1844-1925) below a gold crown within a white enamel and gold frame, with vacant compartment in original red velvet fitted case-1 1/8 in. long

Born Alexandra Caroline Mary Charlotte Louisa Julia, Princess of Schleswig-Holstein-Sonderburg-Glücksburg (the reigning house of the Kingdom of Denmark), Princess Alexandra was queen consort of King Edward VII of Great Britain. Her younger sister, Princess Dagmar (Maria Fedorovna), wed the future Emperor Alexander III of Russia.

Provenance:

Purchased from S.J. Shrubsole, New York

Estimate: $2,500 - $3,500

The Russo Collection is being sold without consignor reserves. All lots will open at 50% of the low estimate.

Session Two, Auction #5003 | Thursday, April 24, 12:00 PM CT   103

36138

Queen Victoria Commemorative Brooch

English, circa 1880, stamped 10ct

Oval, the center with an enameled portrait of Queen Victoria (r. 1837-1901) facing left, *églomisé* on a red enameled background, the blue enameled oval border forming the Order of the Garter, inscribed in gold *HONI SOIT QUI MAL Y PENSE*, the reverse engraved *WAKERY, LONDON*, for the portrait photographer on which this image is based-1 7/8 in. long, in original red velvet fitted box stamped *R.L. Christie Jeweller & Watchmaker, 17,18,19,20 Bank St. Edinburgh*

Provenance:

Purchased from Morning Glory, New York

Estimate: $4,000 - $6,000

36139

Queen Victoria Portrait Miniature Mounted as a Gold Bracelet

English, circa 1850

Depicting a young Queen Victoria (r. 1837-1901), her head and shoulders slightly to sinister, dressed *à la Grec* wearing a neo-classical diadem with upswept hair, pendant earrings, and a gold necklace, her pale blue dress with lace border, on a turquoise background, the miniature watercolor set within a scrollwork gold frame forming a locket attached to an engraved, articulated gold bracelet-miniature within frame-1 3/4 in.; length of bracelet-7 1/2 in. long, in original fitted case

Provenance:

Purchased from Morning Glory, New York

Estimate: $4,000 - $6,000

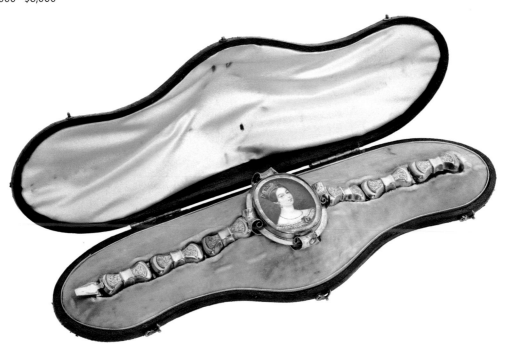

Victorian Diamond, Pearl, and Enameled Gold Royal Presentation Brooch

English, circa 1880

Forming the entwined initials *VRI* for Victoria, Regina et Imperatrix (Queen and Empress), the *RI* initials set with rose diamonds, the *V* set with 24 graduated pearls measuring 1.8 to 4.00 mm, below a red enameled gold rose-cut diamond Royal British crown, mounted in gold-2 1/8 in long

36141

Queen Victoria Gold and Pearl Royal Presentation Bangle Bracelet

English, circa 1885, retailed by Garrard's, London

Designed as a tapered polished gold bangle, the front with oval photograph of the queen, surrounded by eighteen pearls (not tested) averaging approximately 5 mm, the reverse engraved *From Victoria, 1885*, photograph within pearl frame-1 in. long, in original silk-lined blue velvet box of issue, stamped *R. S. Garrard & Co. Goldsmiths & Jewellers to the Crown, 25 Haymarket, London*

Victoria (1819-1901)

Great Britain's longest reigning monarch, Queen Victoria gave her name to the era that saw her Kingdom reach the pinnacle of power and prosperity. Indeed, her popularity probably saved the British monarchy from abolition. Born Alexandrine Victoria of Hanover in 1819, she was only 18 when she acceded to the throne in 1837. Queen Victoria took Prince Albert of Saxe-Coburg-Gotha as her consort on 10 February 1840. This marriage, which ended with his death in 1861 at the age of 42, produced nine children through whose marriages many of Europe's royal houses are descended. Victoria was also given the title Empress of India in 1876.

Provenance:

Presented by Victoria, Queen of Great Britain and Empress of India, to Lady Mary Augusta Frederic Grimstone, wife of the 4th Earl of Radnor.

Purchased from The Armoury of St. James, London

Estimate: $6,000 - $8,000

The Russo Collection is being sold without consignor reserves. All lots will open at 50% of the low estimate.

36142

Edward VII Diamond and Enamel Royal Presentation Stickpin

Circa 1902

Designed as an oval royal blue enamel plaque applied with the gold initial *E VII* for Edward VII, King of Great Britain and Emperor of India (r. 1901-1910), surrounded by gold laurel leaves and berries enhanced with nine graduated old mine-cut diamonds measuring 2.5 to 4.5 mm, below a Royal British crown, the gold reverse inscribed *Presented by his late majesty King Edward VII on the occasion of the performance of " A Cigarette Makers Romance" at Sandringham January 11th, 1902*-enameled plaque-7/8 in long; the pin-2 1/4 in. long

Edward VII (1841-1910)

If Queen Victoria saved the British monarchy from possible abolition, her eldest son, Albert Edward of Saxe-Coburg-Gotha, restored its popularity. An affable monarch and an excellent judge of men, the King was much more outgoing than his mother, who had become somewhat withdrawn upon the death of her consort, Prince Albert. Edward's name was bestowed on an era nostalgically remembered by Britons for its opulence and confidence.

Provenance:

Given by King Edward VII to Mr. Martin Harvey, who with his wife and company performed "The Cigarette Maker's Romance" at Sandringham on the 11th of January, 1902. It was staged in the Ball Room in the presence of the King and Queen, the Prince and Princess of Wales and Princess Victoria, and a number of local dignitaries.

Purchased from Sandra Cronan Ltd., London

Estimate: $4,000 - $6,000

Edward VII enameled Gold and Sapphire Royal Presentation Pendant/Brooch

English, circa 1905

Designed as a white enameled openwork star enclosing the entwined initials *ER VII* for King Edward VII
(r. 1901-1910) set with rose diamonds and small rubies, framed by seven cabochon sapphire collets averaging
approximately 3.7 mm, mounted in gold as an adjustable brooch and pendant-1 3/4 in. long

Literature:

Philip Ziegler, *Mountbatten, The Official Biography* (London: Collins, 1985) pp. 34, 101.

Provenance:

Given by King Edward VII to Princess Alice of Greece (1885-1969), eldest Child of Prince Louis of Battenburg (cr.
Marques of Milford Haven 1917) and Princess Victoria of Hesse-Darmstadt (1863-1950); a great granddaughter
of Queen Victoria; elder sister of Louis, Viscount Mountbatten of Burma; mother of the Duke of Edinburgh; and
mother-in-law to the Queen Elizabeth of Great Britain.

Purchased from The Armoury of St. James, London

36144

Rare French Enameled Gold and Diamond Royal Presentation Bracelet

Circa 1850, stamped with eagle head poinçons and Paris lozenge mark

The center segment of cartouche outline decorated with royal blue *guilloché* enamel in a sunray pattern and an openwork scrolling foliate design, framing a central nine-pointed diamond-set coronet, with additional graduated curved panels of scrollwork decorated with blue enamel and set with eight small diamonds, attached to a intricately engraved gold clasp-approximately 7 in. long.

Said to be from the family of the Comte de Paris, pretender to the throne of France. The last King of the royal house of Bourbon-Orléans, Louis-Philippe, abdicated during the Revolution of 1848. While adopting the title of prince, his heirs style themselves Count of Paris.

Provenance:

Purchased from Sheldon Shapiro, London

Estimate: $6,000 - $8,000

Rare Chinese Gold Imperial Necklace

Work of the Symbol of the Empress of China, most likely the Empress Dowager Cixi, circa 1870

Designed as a row of 22 karat gold oval and shaped rectangular plaques, each applied with filigreed three-dimensional phoenixes, attached by a double-link chains, central plaque-1 1/2 in wide; approx length 17 in., in fitted case

Cixi (1835-1908)

A low-ranking concubine to China's Xianfeng Emperor, Cixi (or Tz'u-hsi) bore his only son, who would reign as Tongzhi. From the beginning of Tongzhi's rule as a young boy in 1861, through her own death 47 years later, the Empress Dowager maintained an iron grip on the Qing (Manchu) dynasty. A figure of considerable notoriety, Cixi was one of the most powerful women in Chinese history.

The phoenix (feng-huang) is the second of the four miraculous creatures of Chinese tradition and symbolized the Empress.

Provenance:

Purchased from Sheldon Shapiro, London

36146

German Gold Brooch with Images of Prince William of Prussia and his Wife

Circa 1881

Set within an intricate gold frame enhanced with sapphires, surmounted by a crown with ribbon below a line of small rose-cut diamonds, enclosing the portrait images of Prince Frederick, William Victor Albert von Hohenzollern, future Emperor of Germany (r. 1888-1918), and his consort Princess Augusta-Victoria of Schleswig-Holstein-Sondernburg-Augustenburg (1858-1921), with rose gold back, probably commemorating the marriage in 1881 of the Imperial couple-1 1/4 in diam.

Estimate: $800 - $1,200

36147

Fine Franz Josef Miniature Gold Enameled Imperial Collar Formed as a Bracelet

Viennese, circa 1849

Designed as the Grand Cross in white and red enamel, centered on the initials *FJ*, for Franz-Josef, Emperor of Austria (r. 1848-1916), King of Hungary (r. 1867-1916), the reverse in white enamel with date *1849* in gold, suspended from a gold link bracelet decorated with eleven alternating enameled circular links, these links decorated either with red initials *FJ* on polished gold, or with gold Habsburg crowns on white ground, enameled on both sides, attached at one end to a gold replica of the star of the order with suspension hook, the reverse engraved *VIRIBUS UNITIS* (by joint effort), the other end with oval link chain-8 1/4 in long, in original fitted gray leather presentation box stamped *C.F. ROTHE K.K. HOF u. KAMMER-JUWELIER, KOHLMARKT I WIEN*

Franz Josef (1830-1916)

One of Europe's longest reigning monarchs, Franz-Joseph was Emperor of Austria, Apostolic King of Hungary, and King of Bohemia from 1848 to 1916. His lengthy rule was marked by tragedy, including a loveless marriage, the suicide and murder of two heirs, and the empire's entry into a disastrous war. His dynasty, the House of Habsburg, survived his death by two years and was replaced by a republic at the end of the First World War, in 1918.

Provenance:

Probably made to commemorate the Coronation of Emperor Franz-Joseph of Austria.

Purchased from Bathgate Ltd., London

Estimate: $2,500 - $3,500

36148

**Kaiser William Commemorative Silver Bracelet
with Portrait Miniatures**

German, stamped 800

Designed as a silver bracelet with separate images of the Emperor and his six sons, each within oval frames, the central link depicting William II, Emperor of Germany (r. 1888-1918) within a silver frame of laurel leaves below the Imperial Hohenzollern crown, flanked on each side by three smaller miniatures, to his right, of Princes William, Frederick and Albert, and to his left, Princes August William, Oscar and Joachim, each attached to a silver link back chain-7 1/2 in. long

Estimate: $2,000 - $3,000

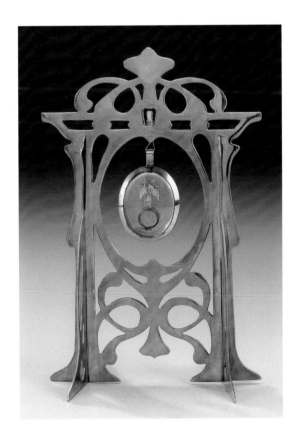

36149

Framed Lock Said to Be of Napoleon's Hair

An oval pendant locket covered with glass on both sides, enclosing a lock of hair encircling the initial *N* for Napoleon Bonaparte, Emperor of France, King of Italy (r. 1804-14), above a French Imperial Eagle, the frame suspended from an Arts & Crafts style brass openwork stand-the locket- 2 in. high; the stand- 7 ¼ in. high

Provenance:

Purchased from The Armoury of St. James, London

Estimate: $800 - $1,000

The Russo Collection is being sold without consignor
reserves. All lots will open at 50% of the low estimate.

Session Two, Auction #5003 | Thursday, April 24, 12:00 PM CT   113

36151

Seymour Lucas (British, 1890-20th Century)

Portrait of Edward VIII, Prince of Wales

Lithograph, signed and dated in the stone

And inscribed *Edward P* and *1911*

22 ½ x 18 in.- framed

Provenance:
Purchased from Hope & Glory, London

Estimate: $200 - $300

36150

William A. Mac Donald (British, 1861-1948)

Coronation of George V, King of Britain, June 22, 1911

Oil on board, signed *W.A.M.* and dated L/R

13 x 9 ½ in.- framed

Provenance:
Purchased from David Broker Fine Art, CT

Estimate: $3,000 - $5,000

36152

Embroidered Military Insignia of King William IV

A military embroidered insignia of William IV, King of Britain
(r. 1830-1837) worked in gold threads on velvet, framed in
mahogany shadowbox, 9 x 9 x 2 in.

Provenance:
Purchased from Forsyth's, Nashville, TN

Estimate: $200 - $300

36153

Fragment of a Piece of the Royal Standard from King William IV's Yacht, *The Royal Adelaide*

Circa 1830

Circular, with a period gilded frame, with Royal Coat of Arms, quartered with central shield embroidered on silk, the reverse of frame with label *Dimensions of His Majesty's Yacht, the Royal Adelaide*-8 1/2 in. long including frame

William IV (1765-1837)

King George III's third son, William Henry of Hanover, entered the Royal Navy as a youth and saw service during the American Revolution and in the West Indies. He was equally active onshore, producing no less than ten illegitimate children by one Irish actress alone before taking the hand of Princess Adelaide of Saxe-Meiningen, after whom he named his yacht. The "Sailor King" reigned from 1830 to 1837. He did not produce any (legitimate) male heirs and was succeeded by his niece, Princess Victoria.

Provenance:
Purchased from The Armoury of St. James, London

Estimate: $1,200 - $1,500

36154

British George IV Windsor Castle Oak and Silver Box

Circa 1825

An oak hinged cigar box, the cover carved with a ribbon-tied laurel garland enclosing the inscription on silver *The Old Oak of Windsor Castle Built by Edward IV and Restored by George IV, J. B.* -6 ¼ in. wide

George IV (1762-1830)

King George IV succeeded his father, George III in 1820, although he had already ruled as regent for nine years because of the latter's insanity. Even by the standards of the day, the future king enjoyed a dissolute youth, having been, as he put it himself, "rather too fond of women and wine." He maintained his indulgent ways into adulthood; in 1827, his corset had a waist of 50 inches. An enthusiastic patron of the arts and architecture, George commissioned, among others, the Royal Pavilion at Brighton Beach, an extravagant Orientalist fantasy.

Estimate: $300 - $400

The Russo Collection is being sold without consignor reserves. All lots will open at 50% of the low estimate.

Session Two, Auction #5003 | Thursday, April 24, 12:00 PM CT   115

36155

George IV Mahogany Sugar Crusher with Provenance Note

The turned handle with a flat base, attached to two period labels of provenance-5 ¾ in. long

Estimate: $300 - $400

36156

British Queen Anne Leather Fan Box

Early 18th century

The reddish-brown morocco case of oval section in two parts, the top displaying the crowned monogram of Anne, Queen of England, Scotland, and Ireland (r. 1702-1714), second daughter of James Duke of York, the edges enhanced with gilded foliage fretwork and beading-9 ¼ in. long

Provenance:

Purchased from Forsyth's, Nashville, TN

Estimate: $700 - $900

36157

A Coronation Commemorative of King Edward VII and Queen Alexandra

Circa 1901

A shadowbox containing the painted full-length bisque figures of Edward and Alexandra, King and Queen of Britain (r. 1901-1910) hands united, overall, 27 x 19 x 4 in.

Provenance:
Purchased from Gray's Market, London

Estimate: $800 - $1,200

36159

British George V Copper Coronation Parade Torch

Circa 1910

A tapered copper torch with leather strap and rivets, the center with coronation inscription, attached to a wooden baluster handle-18 in. long

Provenance:

Purchased from Hope & Glory, London

Estimate: $150 - $250

36158

English George VI Coronation Brass Lantern Clock

1937

In the Old German style with French decorative elements, the dial decorated with the English coat of arms in enamel, flanked by the initials *GVI* and *R,* for *George VI, Rex,* commemorating the coronation of George VI, King of Great Britain (r. 1936-52), the bell in the form of the British Royal crown with a gilt movement, a platform lever escapement, single strike on the hour, signed *Made in England*-11 ½ in. high

Provenance:

Purchased from Camden Passage, London

Estimate: $200 - $300

36160

British George V and Queen Mary Jubilee Panorama

1935

Designed as a cylindrical case on a flat base containing a panoramic scroll which unfurls to display a royal cortège advancing before Buckingham Palace, captioned: *Captain's Escort of Royal Horse Guards, the Duke and Duchess of York, Princess Elizabeth, Princess Margaret Rose of York, the Duke and Duchess of Kent, Escort of Royal Horse Guards,* the exterior depicting in the round the British Royal Family and its entourage, below the inscription *Panorama of the Silver Jubilee,* with the crowned initials *G.R. and M.R. 1935* in Latin numerals-7 ½ in. high

Provenance:

Purchased from Lyme Regis, New York

Estimate: $250 - $450

The Russo Collection is being sold without consignor reserves. All lots will open at 50% of the low estimate.

Session Two, Auction #5003 | Thursday, April 24, 12:00 PM CT   117

36161

Queen Victoria Jubilee Needlepoint Bag with Royal Coat of Arms of the United Kingdom

1887

For the Golden Jubilee, in the form of a shield embroidered in bright colors against a burgundy ground within black beaded borders, attached to an oval link chain-the bag- 9 in. long

Estimate: $400 - $600

36162

Pair of Queen Victoria Jubilee Brass-Mounted Bellows

1887

Made to honor Queen Victoria's Golden Jubilee, one side decorated with a *repoussé* portrait bust of the British Queen, the border with dedication inscription-15 in. long

Provenance:

Purchased from Hope & Glory, London

Estimate: $300 - $500

36163

Queen Victoria Diamond Jubilee Ceremonial Spade

1897

With oak handle mounted on a silver-plated brass spade with dedication inscription, dated June 22nd, 1897, the handle and border decorated with oak leaves-36 in. long

Provenance:

Purchased at James Robinson, New York

Estimate: $2,000 - $3,000

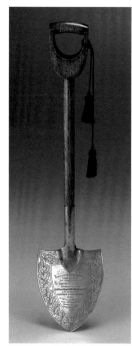

36164

Victorian Bronze *Doré* Inkwell in the Form of the English Royal Crown to Commemorate Queen Victoria's Diamond Jubilee

English, circa 1897

The circular hinged inkwell opening to reveal a round rock crystal ormolu mounted ink jar, the hinged cover with initials *VR* for Victoria Regina, with original red velvet contained inside crown-the inkjar-2 1/2 in. diam.; the crown- 6 in. high

Provenance:

Purchased from Copley South Antiques

Estimate: $2,000 - $3,000

The Russo Collection is being sold without consignor reserves. All lots will open at 50% of the low estimate.

Session Two, Auction #5003 | Thursday, April 24, 12:00 PM CT   119

36165

Three British Commemorative Figural Pipes

One of burlwood carved with the head of King Edward VII (r. 1901-1910)-6 ½ in.; and a pair of miniature meerchaum pipes of King George V (r. 1910-1936) and Queen Mary-2 ¼ and 3 in. respectively

Estimate: $500 - $800

36166

Edward VII, Prince of Wales, Personal Ink Blotter

1900

The red velvet folder, having gold and silver embroidered trim in the Vienna Secessionist style incorporating the Prince of Wales Feathered emblem and the year 1900, 12 1/4 x 15 1/2 in.

1900 was a propitious year for Edward when he was the victim of an attempted assassination over the Boer War. The following year, he became King at the death of Queen Victoria (r. 1901-1910).

Estimate: $1,500 - $2,000

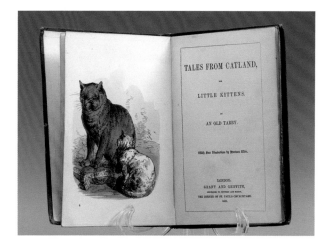

36167

Book Signed by Queen Victoria, Given as a Gift for Christmas, 1851

Hardbound book entitled *Tales From Cat Land,* by an Old Tabby, signed by Victoria, Queen of England (r. 1837-1901), as a Christmas present to her dresser Skirrete, dated December 24, 1851, with illustrations by Harrison Weir, published by Grant and Griffith, London, 1851, with green leatherette embossed cover with gilt tooling, 7 x 5 in.

Estimate: $200 - $300

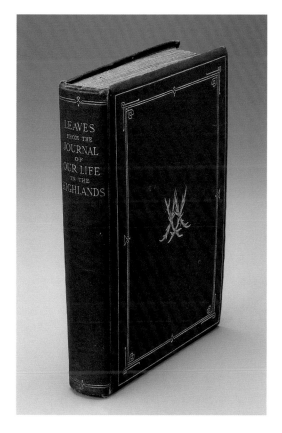

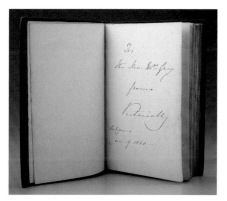

36168

Book Signed by Queen Victoria

Leatherbound book entitled *Leaves From The Journal of Our Lives,* signed on the frontispiece by Victoria, Queen of England, (r. 1837-1901), to the Hon. William Grey, edited by Arthur Helps, published by Smith, Elder & Co, London, with green leatherette binding with gold tooling, 8 ½ x 6 x 2 in.

Provenance:

Purchased from Argosy Books, New York

Estimate: $200 - $300

The Russo Collection is being sold without consignor reserves. All lots will open at 50% of the low estimate.

Session Two, Auction #5003 | Thursday, April 24, 12:00 PM CT   121

36169

Three Musical Scores from the Library of Alexandra, Queen Consort of Britain

Red leatherette musical scores from the Royal library, having Queen Alexandra Royal seals, comprising *Mignon,* by A. Thomas; *Hamlet* by A. Thomas, and *Les Diamantes de la Couronne,* by Auber, 11 x 8 in.

Provenance:

Purchased from Camden Passage, London

Estimate: $200 - $300

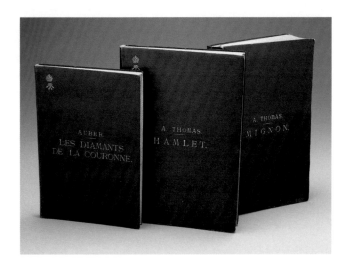

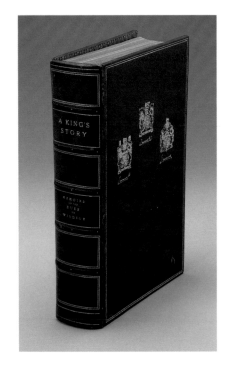

36170

Book Signed by Edward, Duke of Windsor (r. 1936)

Red leatherbound book entitled *A King's Story,* signed by Edward, Duke of Windsor, ghostwritten for the Duke, 1951, published by G.P. Putnam, New York, from an edition limited to 385 copies, red Moroccan leather binding with gilt tooling, 10 x 7 x 3 in.

Provenance:

Purchased at Argosy Books, New York

Estimate: $200 - $300

36171

Admissions Certificate to the Coronation of King George V

For the coronation of George V, King of Great Britain (r. 1910-1936), at Westminster Abbey, in 1911, with Royal embossed seal, in colors, framed, 14 x 15 in.

Provenance:

Purchased from Hope & Glory, London

Estimate: $100 - $150

36172

Original Concert Program Pages for Queen Victoria

Two printed concert listings from Buckingham Palace, June 23, 1871, and July 5, 1866- the date of her daughter Princess Helena's marriage at Windsor Castle, on doily paper stock, both individually framed, 14 x 12 in.

Provenance:

Purchased from Hope & Glory, London

Estimate: $300 - $500

36173

A Pair of Handwritten Menus from Queen Victoria,
(r. 1837-1901)

One from Buckingham Palace, dated March 13, 1890, the other from Osborne, dated January 2, 1896, on Royal paper stock, for Her Majesty, framed, 10 ½ x 7 in.

Provenance:

Purchased from Hope & Glory, London

Estimate: $300 - $500

36174

Original Sheets from the Wedding Announcement of Princess Helena, Daughter of Queen Victoria

Printed frontispiece and page from Queen Victoria's daughter Princess Helena's wedding announcement on doily paper, in Windsor Castle, July 5, 1866, framed together 14 x 21 ½ in.

Provenance:

Purchased from Hope & Glory, London

Estimate: $300 - $500

The Russo Collection is being sold without consignor reserves. All lots will open at 50% of the low estimate.

Session Two, Auction #5003 | Thursday, April 24, 12:00 PM CT   123

36175

Set of Thirteen Victorian Royal Wax Seals

Circa 1880

The red seals displayed in shadowbox frame of birdseye maple, depicting Holland, Siam (2), Italy, Mexico, France (2), Portugal, The Netherlands, Spain, Württemberg, Austria, and Brazil, 16 x 13 ½ in.

Estimate: $300 - $500

36176

Pair of Imperial Austro-Hungarian Painted Wax Figures

Circa 1790

Colorfully painted in enamels, depicting an imperial couple on horseback, with Imperial Austro-Hungarian emblems, framed together, 13 x 21 in.

Estimate: $1,000 - $1,500

Austro-Hungarian Ink Blotter Belonging to Archduke Karl Ludwig Joseph Maria of Austria

Circa 1890

Rectangular, green velvet exterior, beige silk interior, the cover applied with enameled Coat of Arms, mantle and crown, the corners applied with Art Nouveau green pink and white floral decoration-16 x 12 1/4 in.

Archduke Karl Ludwig Joseph Maria von Habsburg-Lotharingen (1833-1896) was the brother of Franz-Joseph, Emperor of Austria (r. 1848-1916). The assassination of Franz-Josef's son, Archduke Franz-Ferdinand, in Sarajevo on June 28, 1914 eventually led to the outbreak of World War I.

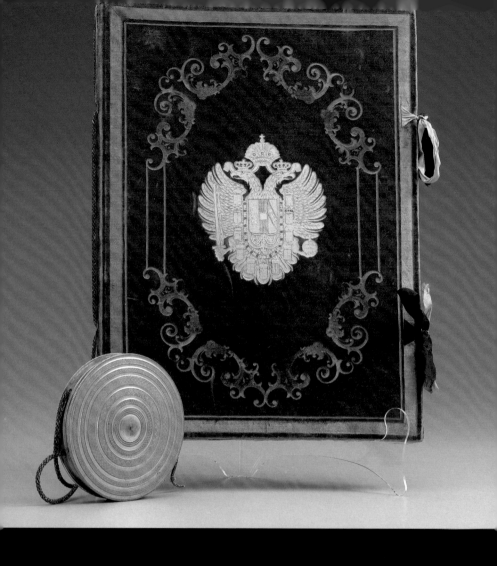

Fine Austro-Hungarian Franz Josef Portfolio Containing Patent of Nobility for Henrich Ritter von Lebzeltern with Attached Seal

Franz Joseph I, Emperor of Austria (1830-1916) Patent of Nobility and Grant of Arms, the covers of red velvet, each side embossed with the Austro-Hungarian double-headed eagle with ribbon ties, containing seven documents in German, some double sided, one with hand painted coat of arms, one signed, the spine

36179

Royal Frederick the Great Brass Commemorative Tobacco Box

By I.H. Giese, Iserlohn, Germany, mid 18th century

Oblong, the hinged cover embossed with the half length figure of Frederick, King of Prussia (r. 1740-1786) turned to the left, his head facing the viewer with Latin inscriptions and a Royal Prussian eagle, the entwined initials *FR* for *Frederick Rex* above with crown and further Latin inscription, the reverse depicting numerous victories including *Leipzig, Friedberg, Neiss,* and *Colberg*, each within oval medallions depicting armies in battle, further enhanced with the Prussian Eagle above the crowned insignia of the King-6 3/8 x 2 x 1 1/4 in.

Frederick II ("The Great") (1712-1786)

Prussia's most celebrated monarch, Frederick was declared King of Prussia at the age of 28. A Francophile and a correspondent of Voltaire, he tried to style himself as the ideal Enlightened monarch, modelling his court at Sans-Souci on Louis XIV's Versailles. Frederick most important legacy, however, was military. His territorial ambitions resulted in a lengthy struggle with Austria. While he succeeded in wresting the wealthy province of Silesia from the Habsburgs, the King's aggression resulted in the Seven Years War. Defeat by Russia was barely averted when Empress Elizabeth was succeeded by her Prussophile son, Peter III. Nevertheless, Frederick was instrumental in raising Prussia to great power status.

Provenance:

Purchased from Suchow & Siegel

Estimate: $1,500 - $2,500

36180

Imperial Austro-Hungarian Enameled, Silver-Plated, and Mahogany Ceremonial Staff

Circa 1900, by Wurtembergisches Metallwaren Fabrik, marked: WMF, Alpacca, O, Z g

The orb-shaped finial with crowned eagle surmount, on a wooden staff with silver-plated tip and hand mount, 58 in. high

Provenance:

Purchased from The Armoury of St. James, London

Estimate: $2,000 - $4,000

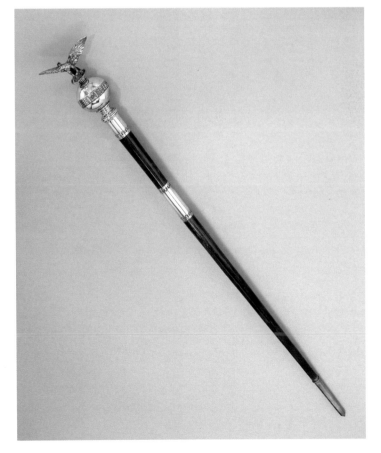

The Russo Collection is being sold without consignor reserves. All lots will open at 50% of the low estimate.

Session Two, Auction #5003 | Thursday, April 24, 12:00 PM CT   127

36181

Minton George VI Porcelain Coronation Loving Cup

1937

Cylindrical, commemorating the coronation of King George VI and Queen Elizabeth , inscribed *Crowned in Westminster Abbey, May 12, 1937,* the reverse with the Royal Coat of Arms, the interior of lip inscribed *King George VI and Queen Elizabeth,* with gilded lion handles-4 ½ in. high

Estimate: $100 - $150

36182

Paragon Queen Elizabeth II Porcelain Coronation Loving Cup

1953

Cylindrical, one side decorated with the Royal Coat of Arms above the inscription *Dieu et Mon Droit,* the reverse with the crowned initials *ER II, H.M. Queen Elizabeth Coronation, June 2nd 1953,* each within a gilded frame of oak leaves on a burgundy ground decorated with a lattice of fleur de lis and rosettes, with gilded scroll handles-4 ¼ in. high

Estimate: $100 - $200

36183

Minton George VI and Queen Elizabeth Porcelain Royal Visit Cup

1939

Cylindrical, a loving cup commemorating the King and Queen's visit to Canada and the United States in 1939, one side decorated with the British Royal crown within a wreath and flags of the commonwealths, the reverse with the Royal Coat of Arms, the interior of lip inscribed *King George VI and Queen Elizabeth,* with gilded lion handles-5 ¾ in. high

Estimate: $400 - $600

36184

Large British Royal Doulton George V and Queen Mary Silver Jubilee Loving Cup

1935

One side of the two-handled cup depicting the royal couple below the words *Happy and Glorious* surrounded by various flags and shields amidst tolling bells, lions passants, jubilant onlookers, and trumpeters, the reverse featuring a knight on horseback, the handles and border decorated with ribbon entwined laurel leaves, number 752 out of 1,000 made, sold together with the original Royal Doulton Certificate with seal, -10 in. high

Estimate: $400 - $600

36185

Copeland Spode Queen Victoria Porcelain Commemorative Boer War Three-handled Loving Cup

1899

Cylindrical, one side with the profile bust of Queen Victoria, inscribed *Victoria Queen and Empress, Comforter of the Afflicted*, surrounded by the Union Jack and flags and seals of the above the motto *Equal Rights for All*, another side decorated with the portraits of the Commander in Chief, Field Marshall Lord Roberts, and the Prime Minister, The Marquis of Salisbury, the third side with a full length figure of Britannia being welcomed by a kneeling South African farmer and the inscription *Britannia Tower of Justice, Defender of the Oppressed*, the interior of cup around the border decorated with further names on ribbons, on a gilded base-5 ½ in. high

Estimate: $250 - $350

The Russo Collection is being sold without consignor reserves. All lots will open at 50% of the low estimate.

Session Two, Auction #5003 | Thursday, April 24, 12:00 PM CT   129

36186

British Ceramic Coronation Figure of George VI

Circa 1936

The full-length figure of George VI, King of Great Britain (1936-1952) in ermine-trimmed coronation robes, wearing the order of the garter and holding the royal crown, a globe with the British Empire designated in red on his right side-8 in. high

Estimate: $200 - $250

36187

Staffordshire George V Ceramic Toby Mug

by Sir Francis Carruthers Gould, Wilkinson, circa 1915

A WWI period character jug of George V, King of England in full naval dress uniform, the sides displaying the Union Jack and the British Royal Coat of Arms, the arm rests in the form of gilded lion heads, a globe on his lap, on a plinth inscribed *Pro Patria*, signed *FCG* -12 in. high

Estimate: $700 - $900

A 19.5% Buyer's Premium applies to all lots.
Visit HA.com/FineArt to view scalable images and bid online.

36188

Biscuit Figure of Edward, Prince of Wales

Circa 1922

After Bryant Baker, the smiling full-length figure wearing tails and a top hat and sporting a tortoiseshell cane, standing on a square pedestal, the front inscribed "Our Prince"-10 ¼ in.

Provenance:

Purchased from Hope & Glory, London

Estimate: $250 - $350

36189

Edward VIII Crystal Coronation Covered Compote

In clear crystal, the circular bowl with scroll handles, a baluster stem on a square plinth, the bowl etched on one side:

Birth June 23rd 1894

By Earth, Sea or Air

Our King Leads the Way

As Friend of His People

They Crown Him Today

And on the other:

Accession January 20, 1936

The Coronation of Edward VIII

King Emperor

May 12, 1937

On a base etched on each side *For England Or Scotland, For Ireland Or Wales*, the domed cover etched with the crowns and names of the eight previous British monarchs named Edward beginning with *Edward I 272* and ending with *Edward VII 1901*-11 in. high

Provenance:

Purchased from Antiquaires du Louvre, Paris

Estimate: $800 - $1,000

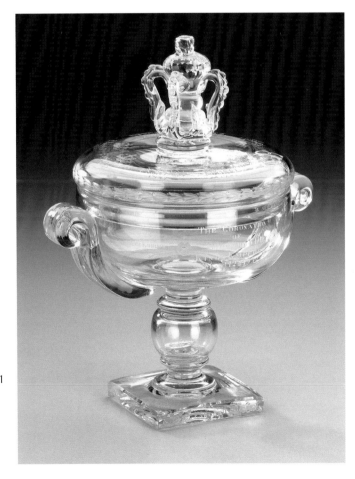

The Russo Collection is being sold without consignor reserves. All lots will open at 50% of the low estimate.

Session Two, Auction #5003 | Thursday, April 24, 12:00 PM CT   131

36190

Queen Victoria Royal Worcester Ceramic Commemorative Scent Flask

Circa 1840

Circular, depicting the profile of the Sovereign facing left on golden background below laurel band, the silvered metal stopper in the form a Royal British crown, the reverse with rose and thistles and shamrocks, the sides decorated with raised flowers-3 in. long

Estimate: $1,500 - $2,000

36191

Pair of Royal Minton Bone China Candlesticks Commemorating Silver Jubilee of Queen Elizabeth II

1977, with maker's stamp on base and inscribed 1952 The Queen's Silver Jubilee 1977, no. 76 of a limited edition of 250

Designed as "Beasts," symbolizing the ancient chivalrous ancestry of the British crown (see lot no. 36192), comprising a White Horse and a Gilt Lion, each rearing on hind legs, the front of Horse with Royal seal, the Lion with red and blue quartered shield, each on spreading white circular base enhanced with royal emblems including fleurs de lis, crown, and Maltese cross with bands of red and gilt-6 in. high

Provenance:
Purchased from Hope & Glory, London

Estimate: $800 - $1,200

36192

The Queen's Beast: A Series of Ten Bone China Figural Ornaments

By Minton China Works, Stoke on Trent, 1955

Each symbolizing the ancient chivalrous ancestry of the British crown, made from the original model of the Queen's vase designed in 1954 by Mr. James Woodford to commemorate the Coronation of Queen Elizabeth II on June 2nd 1953, the production of these individual figures issued in 1955 was limited to six months:

The White Lion of Mortimer, in silver holding blue and mulberry red shield of livery of the House of York

The Lions of England, gold wearing a royal crown and bearing shield showing Royal crown of the U.K

The Unicorn of Scotland, white with hoofs, horn mane, and tufts in gold, shield bears Royal Arms of Former Scottish Kings

The White Horse of Hanover white, bears shield of Royal Arms of the U.K.

The White Greyhound of Richmond, red collar with shield of Tudor livery in white and green

The Red Dragon of Wales, red with yellow underside, shield associated with shield.

The Yale of Beaufort, a silver goat with golden spots with divided white and blue shield bearing crowned portcullis

The Falcon of the Plantagenets, silver with outspread wings, golden legs and beak, shield with livery colors of the House of York

The Black Bull of Clarence, golden hoofs and horns holding shield of Royal arms as borne by English Sovereigns (1405-1603)

The Griffin of Edward III, gold, bears shield of present royal livery colors, red and gold with Round Tower of Windsor Castle

Each with royal Minton stamp on base and name of figure, on white bases-6 in. high, in original fitted box stamped *The Queen's Beasts, Minton ltd.*, with royal warrant.

The original purchase price for one figure (boxed) was 17 pounds 10 shillings or for a complete set of ten, 175 pounds, a considerable sum in 1955.

Provenance:
Purchased from Hope & Glory, London

Estimate: $3,500 - $5,500

The Russo Collection is being sold without consignor reserves. All lots will open at 50% of the low estimate.

Session Two, Auction #5003 | Thursday, April 24, 12:00 PM CT   133

36193

Pair of Copeland Spode George V Ceramic Coronation Bottles

1911

One of cobalt blue, the other moss green, each bearing the Royal couples portraits on royal banners below the Royal crown, below the inscription *Coronation of King George V & Queen Mary, June 22nd 1911*, the reverse signed *Andrew Usher & Co. Distillers Edinburgh* above with the Royal coat of arms, the stoppers in the form of the Royal crown-9 ½ in. high

Estimate: $200 - $300

36194

Minton Bone China Elizabeth II Covered Box in the Form of an Orb

1953

Of teal blue porcelain decorated with royal emblems, stars below a crown finial, on a spreading gilded base, with central commemorative inscription: *To Commemorate the Crowning of Queen Elizabeth The Second, June 2, 1953*, the base stamped "Limited Issue of 50 of which this is No 8." with makers mark and designer's signature-5 in. diam.

Estimate: $400 - $500

36195

**British George VI and Queen Elizabeth Cup Commemorating Their
Visit to the United States**

1939

Of ovoid form, one side displaying the American National Eagle, the reverse with a
royal portrait of King George VI and Queen Elizabeth, amidst gilded stars below gilded
border decorated with the American eagle alternating with the British Royal crown, on a
columnar base encircled by white eagles with splayed wings, on a spreading base, with
two lion masks handles-8 in. high

Estimate: $300 - $500

36196

Copeland Edward VII Ceramic Coronation Two-handled Cup

1910

Of flared design on a spreading base, featuring the royal portrait bust of
King Edward VII, below the inscription *Edward VII King and Emperor,
Accession January 22, 1901, Born November 9th 1841, died May 6th 1910,*
amidst various other proclamation inscriptions, the reverse with an image
of Peace enthroned flanked by flags, the flared lip with interior inscriptions
on ribbons, with gilded border and foliate handles-6 ¾ in.

Provenance:

Purchased from Gem Antiques, New York

Estimate: $700 - $900

36197

Paragon Queen Elizabeth II Ceramic Coronation Loving Cup

1953

Cylindrical, one side with the crowned initials *ER II*, below the Royal crown
and above the coronation date, further inscribed both in Latin and *Crowned
in Westminster Abbey, June 2nd 1953* on the other, the reverse with the
Royal Coat of Arms above the inscription *Dieu et mon Droit,* the interior of
lip inscribed *Coronation of HM Queen Elizabeth II,* with gilded lion handles-
4 ½ in. high

Estimate: $300 - $500

The Russo Collection is being sold without consignor
reserves. All lots will open at 50% of the low estimate.

Session Two, Auction #5003 | Thursday, April 24, 12:00 PM CT   135

36198

Crown Devon Fieldings Edward VIII Ceramic Abdication Mug

1936

One side depicting the portrait of Edward VIII below the Royal crown, surrounded by flags of the commonwealth and the Union Jack, the reverse with crown and inscription *Long May He Reign* above the lyrics for the National Athem, and the abdication date of December 10th 1936, the spreading base with floral garland, the handle decorated with oak leaves and flowerheads-6 ¼ in. high

Estimate: $200 - $300

36199

Royal Doulton Edward VIII Ceramic Loving Cup

1936

One side depicting the profile bust of the monarch in full court dress under the motto *God Save the King*, surrounded by flags of the commonwealth and the Union Jack, the reverse depicting Edward flanked by the Prince of Wales Feathers above the dates *1911-1936*, and the inscription *I am still that same man,* the border inscribed with the names of the commonwealth countries and *Edward RI, Our Prince*-6 in. high

Estimate: $500 - $600

36200

Sèvres Bisque Porcelain Nicholas and Alexandra Medallion Commemorating their Visit to the Factory

French, circa 1896

Of white porcelain, depicting the Imperial couple facing right, he in military uniform, she wearing a *kokoshnik*, inscribed *NICHOLAS II* and *ALEXANDRA*, the reverse inscribed *LL MM L'EMPEREUR ET L'EMPERATRICE DE RUSSIE VISITENT LA MANUFACTURE NATIONALE DE SEVRES, 8 OCTOBRE 1896-* 3 1/2 in. diam. in original red leather box, the top embossed *MANUFACTURE NATIONALE DE SEVRES* and dated

Provenance:

Purchased from St. Petersburg Shop, Paris

Estimate: $3,000 - $5,000

The Russo Collection is being sold without consignor reserves. All lots will open at 50% of the low estimate.

36201

Small German Bisque Porcelain Bust of Queen Victoria

Late 19th century

For Queen Victoria's Diamond Jubilee, the reverse signed signed *R. Belt, Sc, 1897, made in Germany*, mounted on a circular mahogany plinth-6 ¼ in. high

Provenance:

Purchased from Hope & Glory, London

Estimate: $400 - $600

36202

Berlin KPM Kaiser Wilhelm II Ceramic Mug

Circa 1900

Depicting the bust of Wilhelm II, Emperor of Germany, King of Prussia (r. 1888-1918), within a gilded laurel wreath, further enhanced with bands of oak and laurel leaves, with a scrolling gilded handle, on three lion paw feet-5 ¼ in. high including handle

Provenance:

Purchased from Hope & Glory, London

Estimate: $150 - $200

36203

A Porcelain Box in the Form of Franz Joseph

Circa 1910

A figural box of the full-bearded Franz Joseph, Emperor of Austria (r. 1848-1916), King of Hungary (r. 1867-1916) enthroned, wearing ermine robe with imperial collar and crown, orb, and scepter-5 ½ in. high

Estimate: $300 - $400

36204

Signed Document from King William IV

The document on parchment, signed by William IV, King of Great Britain, (r. 1830-1837), dated September 25, 1834, to Anne of London, as a certificate of Registry, with Royal emblems, framed together with a lithograph of the Monarch, 16 x 25 in.

Estimate: $200 - $300

36205

School Exercise Book of Prince George, Future King of Great Britain

The primer with marbelized cover with six pages of English dictation in the hand of the future King George V (r. 1910-1936), as a boy in 1878, and including 13 manuscript pages in another hand regarding the West Indies, 9 x 7 in.

Estimate: $300 - $500

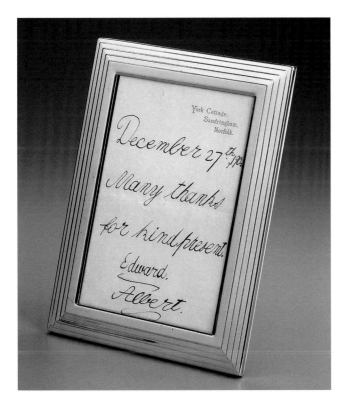

36206

Original Handwritten Personal Letter from Edward VIII and George VI

Prescient note from the two brothers and future Kings of England, (r. 1936- abdication and r. 1936-1852), Written letter signed by both as children, dated December 27, 1902, on York Cottage, Norfolk stationery, reading "Many thanks for your kind present", framed, 6 ½ x 4 ½ in.

Estimate: $1,000 - $1,500

The Russo Collection is being sold without consignor reserves. All lots will open at 50% of the low estimate.

Session Two, Auction #5003 | Thursday, April 24, 12:00 PM CT   139

36207

Signed Document from Queen Victoria

The document signed by Victoria, Queen of Great Britain (r. 1837-1901) and signed by the Duke of Albany, regarding the monarch's appointment as Colonel to the Land Forces, framed together with a hand colored engraving of the Queen, 21 x 32 in.

Estimate: $300 - $500

36208

Queen Victoria Letter and Envelope with Royal Seal

A letter addressed to Ferdinand II, King of the Two Sicilies (r. 1830-1859), announcing the death of her uncle, the Duke of Cambridge, youngest son of King George III, below a photograph of Queen Victoria, the letter dated July 17, 1850 and signed *Sir my Brother, your Majesty & Good Sister Victoria..*, framed; the envelope inscribed *To My Good Brother, The King of the Kingdom of the two Sicilies*, the reverse with royal wax seal, framed-The letter-8 ½ x 6 ¾; frame-18 ½ x 12 ¾; the envelope- 4 ½ x 3 ¾; frame-10 5/8 x 10 in.

Estimate: $3,500 - $4,000

36209

A Written and Signed Postcard from Edward VIII, Prince of Wales, as a boy

The card depicting Windsor Castle, by the Monarch as a child, dated April 13, 1907, to Madame Bricka, thanking her for her previous correspondence, framed together with a photograph of Edward as a boy, 10 ½ x 15 in.

Provenance:

Purchased from Altman's, New York

Estimate: $1,000 - $1,500

36210

Large Christmas Card from King George V

1930 Christmas card, oversize, signed by George V, King of Great Britain (r. 1910-1936) and dated in blue crayon, with a reproduction of the "Loyal London"- one of Charles II's sailing ships, on folded ivory cardstock, with navy grosgrain ribbon, 14 x 10 in.

Estimate: $200 - $300

36211

Christmas Card Signed by Elizabeth II

Circa 1952

Elizabeth, Queen of England (r. 1952-), printed from a photograph by Cecil Beaton, signed, framed, 11 ½ x 7 in.

Estimate: $500 - $700

The Russo Collection is being sold without consignor reserves. All lots will open at 50% of the low estimate.

Session Two, Auction #5003 | Thursday, April 24, 12:00 PM CT   141

36212

A Christmas Card Signed by Elizabeth II and Prince Philip

Christmas card for 1970, signed by the Queen of England (r. 1952-), and her husband Prince Philip, and framed with a printed photograph of the couple, 18 x 14 in.

Provenance:
Purchased from Kenneth Rendell Gallery, New York

Estimate: $500 - $700

36213

Prussian Frederick the Great Military Document with Seal

1778

Intact, signed, framed with contemporary engraving, document-13 x 8 in.; frame-13 x 26 in.

Provenance:
Purchased from Argosy Books, New York

Estimate: $2,500 - $3,500

A 19.5% Buyer's Premium applies to all lots.
Visit HA.com/FineArt to view scalable images and bid online.

36214

Signed Note from Frederick William, Crown Prince of Germany and Prussia

Attractively framed note signed by the Monarch, dated *February 1885, Berlin*, and a card depicting Frederick III (r. 9 March-15 June 1888), by Linde and Scheurich, Berlin, circa 1880, 6 ½ x 4 ¼ in., framed together, 24 x 15 in.

Estimate: $1,000 - $1,500

36215

Signed Photogravure of Emperor William II

Printed photograph of Kaiser William, Emperor of Germany, (r. 1888-1918) by Reichard & Lindner, Berlin, signed by the monarch, and inscribed *Lisbon, March 30, 1905*, in a satinwood trimmed walnut frame with metal bosses at corners, 11 ½ x 8 ½ in.

Provenance:
Purchased from Hope & Glory, London

Estimate: $1,000 - $1,500

36216

Original Coronation Photograph of Queen Alexandra

Circa 1910

The sepia toned photograph of Alexandra, Queen Consort of Britain, Wife of Edward VII, mounted on cardstock and inscribed *Alexandra*, 16 x 12 in.

Provenance:

Purchased from Maggs Bros., London

Estimate: $500 - $700

The Russo Collection is being sold without consignor reserves. All lots will open at 50% of the low estimate.

36217

Original Presentation Photograph of Alexandra, Queen Consort of Britain

A photograph of the Royal family, at Bernstorff, dated October 1902, in Royal yellow silk presentation cover, 7 x 10 in.

Estimate: $300 - $500

36218

Original Photograph of Queen Victoria

Sepia toned photograph of Victoria, Queen of England (r. 1837-1901), inscribed and dated 1885, in a parquetry-trimmed mahogany shadowbox frame, 12 x 10 in.

Provenance:

Purchased from Joseph Topping, Triple Pier Show, New York

Estimate: $300 - $500

36219

King Edward VII *Repoussé* Commemorative Copper Frame

English, circa 1901

Enclosing photographic postcard signed *Russell & Sons Photographers to the Royal Family* depicting the Monarch facing left in 3/4 profile, the image set to the right of the frame below the Royal crown, a lion rampant to the left with entwined ribbon and Latin motto, a fluted column to the right, the decoration raised and *repoussé* from the back with border on the top and bottom, possibly made to commemorate the King's Coronation in 1901-10 x 7 in.

Provenance:

Purchased from Hope & Glory, London

Estimate: $800 - $1,200

36220

Pair of Royal Presentation Silver Frames with Signed Photographs of the Duke and Duchess of Connaught

Early 20th century

The Duke (son of Queen Victoria) shown 3/4 length wearing military uniform orders, sash, cords (riding boots) holding a document, signed *Arthur 1914*, the Duchess in formal court gown wearing ermine robe, diamond tiara and holding royal crown, her arm resting on the back of a chair, signed *Louise Margaret 1914*, each with silver reed-and-tie bordered frame surmounted by the respective crowned initials *AW* and *LM*-Photo of Duchess-7 3/4 x 4 1/2 in.; the Duke-11 x 6 in.; each frame-12 3/4 x 7 1/2 in.

Prince Arthur married Princess Louise Margaret (1860-1917), daughter of Prince Frederick of Prussia, in 1879.

Estimate: $1,500 - $2,000

36221

Royal Presentation King George VI and Queen Elizabeth Silver-Gilt Photograph Frame

Marked Turner & Simpson Ltd. Birmingham, 1939

The silver rectangular frame applied with gold crown enclosing original photograph of the George VI, King of Great Britain (r. 1936-1952) wearing army uniform, strolling with his consort, Queen Elizabeth (1900-2002) who is wearing a light colored dress and overcoat signed *George R. I.* and *Elizabeth R* above the date *1941*-8 x 6 1/4 in.; the frame 11 1/2 x 8 1/2 in.

Estimate: $3,000 - $5,000

The Russo Collection is being sold without consignor reserves. All lots will open at 50% of the low estimate.

Session Two, Auction #5003 | Thursday, April 24, 12:00 PM CT   145

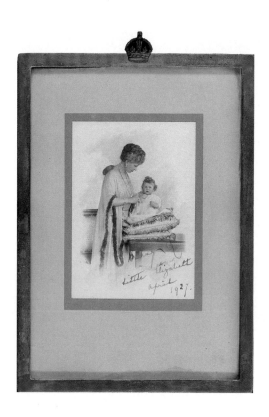

36222

Original Photograph of Queen Mary and Princess Elizabeth

A rare photograph of Mary, Queen of England, with her granddaughter, Crown Princess Elizabeth, as a child, by A.A. Hughes, inscribed with their names, and dated April 1927, 6 ½ x 4 ½ in., framed in Royal gilt wood presentation frame, 12 ½ x 9 in.

Provenance:

Purchased from Maggs Bros., London

Estimate: $500 - $700

36223

Pair of Photogravures of King George V and Queen Mary

Attractive pair of Royal photogravures, signed by George V (r. 1910-1936) and Mary, King and Queen of England, and dated 1920, engraving by W & D Downey, England, mounted on cardstock with Royal emblem, in red leather presentation frames, also with Royal emblems, 15 x 10 in.

Provenance:

Purchased from Sheldon Shapiro, London

Estimate: $800 - $1,200

36224

Pair of Engravings of King George V and Queen Mary

by Downey, England, inscribed *George R.I.* and *Mary R.*, *Waverley Abbey, July 1st, 1916*, framed, 22 x 20 in. each

Provenance:

Purchased from Hope & Glory, London

Estimate: $1,000 - $1,500

36225

Signed Photogravure of Edward, Prince of Wales

The frame marked *Sterling, #420*

Printed photogravure, signed by the future monarch and dated *1919*, in silver presentation frame with Royal Prince of Wales Feathers, having cornflower blue grosgrain ribbon trim, 10 in. high

Provenance:

Purchased at Argosy Books, New York

Estimate: $1,000 - $1,500

The Russo Collection is being sold without consignor reserves. All lots will open at 50% of the low estimate.

Session Two, Auction #5003 | Thursday, April 24, 12:00 PM CT   147

36226

Signed Photograph of Prince Edward, as a Boy

Edward of York, Prince of Wales, (r. 1936, abdicated), seaside portrait photograph of the Prince in a bathing costume and holding a towel, signed *David*, and dated *July 1, 1908*, with inscription *"You never knew about me, I never knew about you. Waiting!!!"* 5 ½ x 3 in. (1/2 inch at top folded over), framed, together with a small cropped photograph of Edward wearing a sailor's suit, inscribed *Baby David*, framed.

The Prince often used David, one of his four first names; the others being George, Andrew, and Patrick. For most of his life, Edward was known to his family and close friends, by his first name, David.

Literature:
"Letters from A Prince", edited by Rupert Godfrey, (1998), London. Illustrated p. 124, Waiting photo; and p. 227, Baby photo.

Provenance:
Freda Dudley Ward, his mistress

Purchased from Maggs Bros., London

Estimate: $800 - $1,200

36227

Original Photograph of Edward, Prince of Wales

Full length photograph in uniform, signed by Edward and dated 1921, in leather presentation frame with the seal of the 10th division of Royal Hussars, framed, 15 x 10 ½ in.

Estimate: $1,000 - $1,500

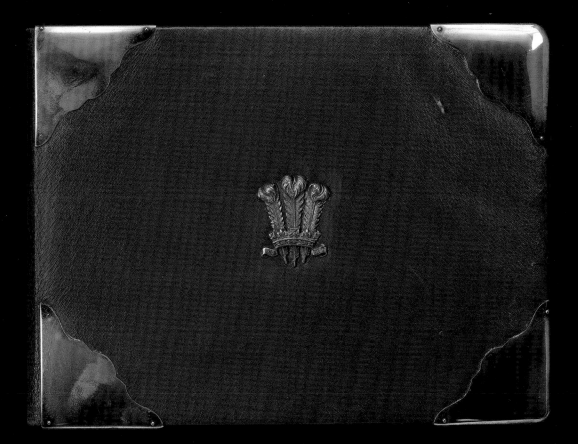

English Silver-mounted Royal Traveling Frame

Marked by the Goldsmiths and Silversmiths Co., London 1926, date letter R

Rectangular portfolio of red morocco, the center applied with silver Prince of Wales Triple Feathers and tooled inside with the Order of the Garter cartouche with Latin motto enclosing monogram *E* for Edward, Prince of Wales, with silver-mounted corners-10 1/8 x 7 1/2 in. Photo pictured is not original.

Edward VIII (1894-1972)

Born Edward Albert Christian George Andrew Patrick David of Saxe-Coburg-Gotha, Edward VIII reigned as King of the United Kingdom of Great Britain and Ireland and Emperor of India for less than a year, from 20 January to 10 December 1936. He abdicated the throne to marry an American divorcée, Wallis Warfield Simpson, and was styled the Duke of Windsor by his successor, King George VI, in 1937.

Provenance:

Edward, Prince of Wales.

Purchased from Marks Antiques, London

PRINCESS DIANA

Framed Photograph of Princess Diana with Signature

Circa 1996

Depicting Diana in a cream colored pearl-encrusted gown, wearing a pearl and diamond tiara and pendant earrings, a separate card with Royal crown signed *Diana*-framed, photo-3 5/8 x 2 ¾ in.; card: 2 x 3 in.; frame: 11 x 7 ½ in.

Provenance:

Purchased from Hope & Glory, London

36230

Three Letters Written by Princess Diana, Prince William, and Prince Henry to Ken Wharfe, Inspector of Police at Kensington Palace

The letters thank him for organizing a private visit to Alton Towers amusement park in 1990, each with original envelopes, Princess Diana's and Prince William's letter on Kensington Palace stationary with crowned insignia *D* for Diana, Princess of Wales (1961-1997), dated October 24, 1990, the latter decorated with red happy faces on the card and envelope, Prince Henry's letter depicting a policeman with his cat, in pencil: *Dear Ken and all the Policemen Thank you for a wonderful day. I loved the Bob sleigh best Love Harry*

Provenance:

Purchased from Hope & Glory, London

Estimate: $7,000 - $9,000

36231

Princess Diana Presentation Frame with Signed Original Photograph of Princess Diana, Prince William, and Prince Henry

Signed and dated Diana 1990

Princess Diana sits with young Prince Henry on her knee while a laughing Prince William stands behind, his arms around Diana, within a textured black rectangular frame with domed top embossed with crowned insignia *D* for Diana, Princess of Wales (1961-1997), in gold-the frame 7 1/2 x 5 3/8 in.; photograph-4 x 3 in.

Provenance:

Commissioned by Princess Diana as a presentation gift.

Purchased from Hope & Glory, London

Estimate: $3,000 - $4,000

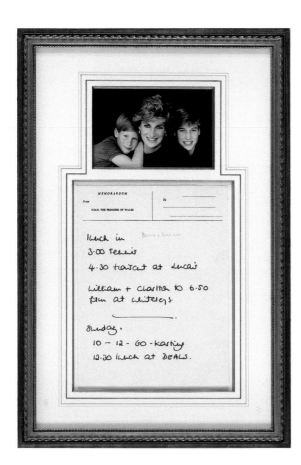

36232

Signed Document from Diana, Princess of Wales

The signed agenda page from and in the hand of Diana Princess of Wales (1961-1997), on her personal stationery, together with a photograph of Princess Diana and her sons, Prince William and Prince Henry-19 x 13 in.

Provenance:

Purchased from Hope & Glory, London

Estimate: $2,000 - $4,000

36233

Prince of Wales Presentation Frame with Signed Original Photograph of Prince Charles and Princess Diana

Signed Diana 1990 Charles

Showing the Prince and Princess of Wales standing together, her arm linked around his, within a textured green rectangular frame, the domed top embossed with Prince of Wales Feathers in gold-the frame- 9 1/2 x 7 in. ; photograph-5 x 4 in.

Provenance:

Commissioned by the Prince and Princess of Wales as a presentation gift

Purchased from Hope & Glory, London

Estimate: $3,000 - $4,000

The Russo Collection is being sold without consignor reserves. All lots will open at 50% of the low estimate.

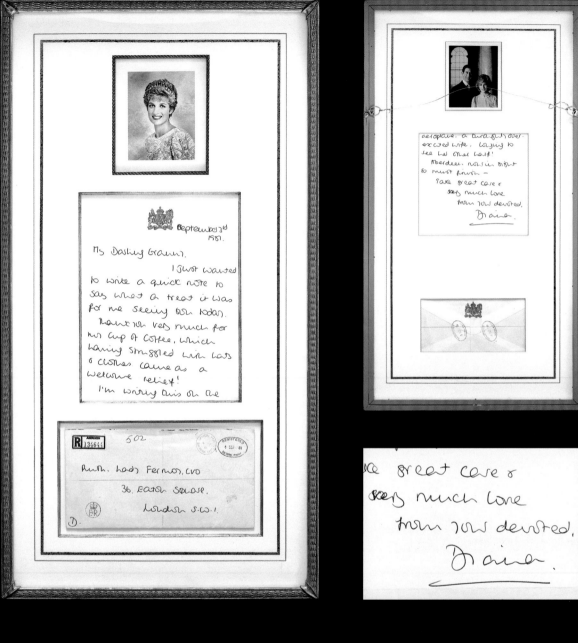

Signed Letter and Envelope from Princess Diana to Her Grandmother

The envelope and letter handwritten on Royal Balmoral Castle stationery by Diana, Princess of Wales, addressed to Ruth Lady Fermot DCVO (Dame Commander of the Royal Victorian Order), regarding their visit and Diana's longing to be reunited with her husband Prince Charles, dated September 3, 1981, framed together with a printed photograph of Diana and the reverse with a Polaroid of the couple Charles and Diana

36235

Two Christmas Cards from Queen Elizabeth and Queen Elizabeth II to Prince Charles and Princess Diana

Two printed Christmas cards, one signed by Queen Elizabeth II and Prince Philip, the cover featuring an image of Queen Elizabeth and the Buckingham Palace Horse Guards, the interior inscribed *Charles and Diana with Love, Mummy, Papa 1986*, the second given by Queen Elizabeth, the Queen Mother, the cover with a Royal Gilt Crown, the interior with an image of the Queen Mother holding flowers, and inscribed *darling Charles and Diana,* and after printed Christmas Greeting: *and much love from Granny,* and dated 1988-6 x 8 ½ in.; 8 5/8 x 7 ½ in.

Provenance:

Purchased from Hope & Glory, London

Estimate: $4,000 - $6,000

The Russo Collection is being sold without consignor reserves. All lots will open at 50% of the low estimate.

Session Two, Auction #5003 | Thursday, April 24, 12:00 PM CT   157

Pair of Princess Diana Blue Enamel and Silver Presentation Cufflinks

London, circa 1990, maker's mark ACB

Designed as oval blue enamel disks decorated with crowned initial *D* for Diana, Princess of Wales (1961-1997),
each attached by a small link chain to a back link of lozenge shape of blue enamel-initialed link 3/4 in. long, with
original blue fitted presentation box, the cover embossed with crowned insignia *D*, the interior stamped with
royal warrants of *Gerald Benney, Berkshire*

Provenance:

Commissioned by Princess Diana as a presentation gift, said to be one of approximately ten pairs made

Purchased from Hope & Glory, London

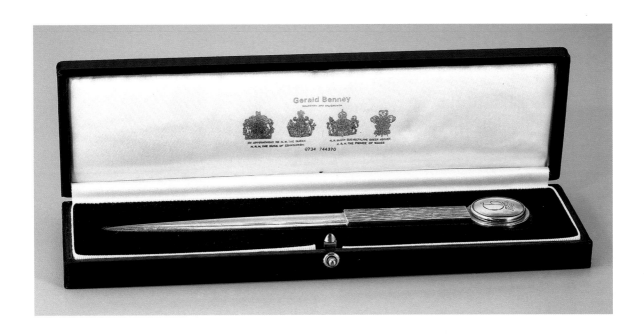

36237

Princess Diana Silver Presentation Paper Knife

London, circa 1990, maker's mark AGB

Of typical form, the tapered polished silver blade enhanced with a textured section simulating wood grain ending in a circular disc engraved with the crowned initial *D* for Diana, Princess of Wales (1961-1997), the reverse with textured sunburst design-7 in. long, in original blue fitted presentation box, the cover embossed with crowned insignia *D,* the interior stamped with royal warrants of *Gerald Benney, Goldsmiths and Jewellers*

Provenance:

Commissioned by Princess Diana as a presentation gift.

Purchased from Hope & Glory, London

Estimate: $3,000 - $5,000

The Russo Collection is being sold without consignor reserves. All lots will open at 50% of the low estimate.

Session Two, Auction #5003 | Thursday, April 24, 12:00 PM CT   159

36238

Pair of Prince of Wales Gold Cufflinks

By Cartier, circa 1990, stamped Cartier London, 375

Designed as double links of oval 9k rose gold disks, each engraved with Prince of Wales Feathers, attached by small gold link chains-3/4 in. long, in original red fitted box stamped *Cartier, London, Paris, New York*

Provenance:

Commissioned by Charles, Prince of Wales (b. 1948) as a presentation gift. Only ten pairs were said to have been made; other pairs were given to Prime Minister John Major, and the Prince's brothers, Andrew, the Duke of York, and Edward, the Earl of Wessex

Purchased from Hope & Glory, London

Estimate: $8,000 - $10,000

THIRD PARTY SHIPPING

Heritage Auction Galleries is now incorporating "**Third Party Shipping**" for select items in our auctions, it shall be the responsibility of the successful bidder to arrange pick up and shipping through a third party, as to such items auctioneer shall have no liability.

- A Third Party Shipper is required on Lots designated as Third Party Shipping.

- An **Agent Shipping Release Authorization Form**, supplied by Heritage Auctions, must be completed, signed and submitted before a Lot can be released for pick up.

- Please allow up to 48 hours for your Lot(s) to be scheduled for a pick up, once we have received your completed Agent Shipping Release Authorization Form.

- The Third Party Shipper and Heritage Auctions' Shipping Department will schedule a day and time to pick up your items.

Choose one of our recommended Third Party Shippers or another of your choice to take delivery of your items. However, you are not obligated to choose from the following and may provide Heritage with information of your preferred shipper.

The UPS Store	**Displays Unlimited Inc.**	**Craters & Freighters**
3818 Cedar Springs Rd, #101	626 106th Street	2450 Merritt Drive
Dallas, TX 75219	Arlington, TX 76011	Garland, TX 75041
Ph: 214-520-0005	Ph: 817-385-4433	Ph: 972-840-8147
Fax: 214-780-5663	Fax: 214-443-8470	Fax: 214-780-5674
store3812@theupsstore.com	transit@displaysunlimitedinc.com	dallas@cratersandfreighters.com

- It is the Third Party Shipper's responsibility to pack (or crate) and ship (or freight) your purchase to you. Please make all payment arrangements for shipping with your Third Party Shipper of choice.

- Any questions concerning Third Party Shipping can be addressed through our Client Services Department at **1-800-872-6467**. For callers outside the U.S., dial **001-214-409-1150**.

MAIL/FAX BID SHEET

Heritage Auction Galleries
Direct Client Service Line — Toll Free: 866-835-3243
For outside U.S., dial (001) 214-409-1150
HA.com
3500 Maple Avenue, 17th Floor
Dallas, Texas 75219-3941
(All information must be completed.)

NAME _____

CUSTOMER # (if known) _____

ADDRESS _____

E-MAIL ADDRESS _____

CITY/STATE/ZIP _____

DAYTIME PHONE (A/C) _____

EVENING PHONE (A/C) _____

Would you like a FAX or e-mail confirming receipt of your bids? If so, please print your FAX # or e-mail address here: _____

REFERENCES: New bidders who are unknown to us must furnish satisfactory industry references or a valid credit card in advance of the sale date.

Dealer References (City, State) and/or Credit Card Information

_____

_____

_____

_____

_____

You are authorized to release payment history information to other dealers and auctioneers so that I may establish proper credit in the industry. (Line out this statement if you do not authorize release.)

Non-Internet bids (including but not limited to, podium, fax, phone and mail bids) may be submitted at any time and are treated similar to floor bids. These types of bids must be on-increment or at a half increment (called a cut bid). Any podium, fax, phone or mail bids that do not conform to a full or half increment will be rounded up or down to the nearest full or half increment and will be considered your high bid.

Current Bid	Bid Increment	Current Bid	Bid Increment
< - $10	$1	$10,000 - $19,999	$1,000
$10 - $29	$2	$20,000 - $29,999	$2,000
$30 - $49	$3	$30,000 - $49,999	$2,500
$50 - $99	$5	$50,000 - $99,999	$5,000
$100 - $199	$10	$100,000 - $199,999	$10,000
$200 - $299	$20	$200,000 - $299,999	$20,000
$300 - $499	$25	$300,000 - $499,999	$25,000
$500 - $999	$50	$500,000 - $999,999	$50,000
$1,000 - $1,999	$100	$1,000,000 - $1,999,999	$100,000
$2,000 - $2,999	$200	$2,000,000 - $2,999,999	$200,000
$3,000 - $4,999	$250	$3,000,000 - $4,999,999	$250,000
$5,000 - $9,999	$500	$5,000,000 - $9,999,999	$500,000
		>$10,000,000	$1,000,000

(Bid in whole dollar amounts only.)

LOT NO.	AMOUNT	LOT NO.	AMOUNT	LOT NO.	AMOUNT	LOT NO.	AMOUNT

PLEASE COMPLETE THIS INFORMATION:

1. IF NECESSARY, PLEASE INCREASE MY BIDS BY:
   ☐ 10%   ☐ 20%   ☐ 30%
   Lots will be purchased as much below bids as possible.

2. ☐ I HAVE BOUGHT COINS FROM YOU BEFORE (references are listed above)

I have read and agree to all of the Terms and Conditions of Auction: inclusive of paying interest at the lesser of 1.5% per month (18% per annum) or the maximum contract interest rate under applicable state law from the date of sale (if the account is not timely paid), and the submission of disputes to arbitration.

_____

(Signature required) Please make a copy of your bid sheet for your records.

SUBTOTAL	
TOTAL from other side	
TOTAL BID	

FAX HOTLINE: (001) 214-409-1425

REV. 01-15-08

LOT NO.	AMOUNT	LOT NO.	AMOUNT	LOT NO.	AMOUNT	LOT NO.	AMOUNT

TOTAL this side

AMOUNT

Please make a copy of your bid sheet for your records.

36239

Magnum of Vintage 1961 Champagne Cuvée Dom Perignon for the Wedding of Charles, Prince of Wales and Lady Diana Spencer

This bottle of champagne was shipped in small quantities to be used for the toast at the wedding breakfast, the Moët et Chandon label reads as follows: *Specially shipped to honour the marriage of His Royal Highness the Prince of Wales and Lady Diana Spencer, 29 July 1981. Champagne Cuvée Dom Perignon, Vintage 1961, Disgorged 1981,* 1961 was the year of Princess Diana's birth

Accompanied with letter by Moet Hennessy dated May 25th 2000 affirming that this Dom Perignon Cuvée was never offered for sale as the quantity at the time of release in 1981 was small.

Provenance:

Presented by Diana, Princess of Wales

Purchased from Hope & Glory, London

Estimate: $20,000 - $30,000

The Russo Collection is being sold without consignor reserves. All lots will open at 50% of the low estimate.

Session Two, Auction #5003 | Thursday, April 24, 12:00 PM CT   161

36240

Silver-Plated Goblet Honoring Charles, Prince of Wales

A sterling silver-plated replica after the original wine chalice for Charles II (r. 1660-1685), to commemorate Charles, Prince of Wales, at Caernarvon Castle, by Preston's, Ltd., dated July 1, 1969, numbered 104 from a limited edition of 1000, in a blue leather fitted presentation case, 6 in. high

Provenance:

Purchased from Hope & Glory, London

Estimate: $200 - $300

36241

Princess Diana Halcyon Days Presentation Carriage Clock

Circa 1990, Hope & Glory Ceramic Specialists, London

The rectangular clock of typical form with chime and polished gilded brass sides, the front panel decorated with light green enamel enhanced with floral clusters, the circular white enamel dial with black Roman chapters, above the crowned initial *D* for Diana, Princess of Wales (1961-1997) within an oval floral frame inscribed *Presented H. R. H. Princess of Wales*; Panel engraved *No. 22* on base. Inscribed *made in England 11 Jewels.*-5 1/8x 3 1/2 x 3 in., in original blue fitted presentation box, the cover embossed in gold with crowned insignia *D*

Produced in very limited numbers; these carriage clocks were usually presented by Princess Diana to a favorite charity as a prestigious gift to raise funds.

Provenance:

Made for Princess Diana

Purchased from Hope & Glory, London

Estimate: $8,000 - $12,000

Lot 36241

The Russo Collection is being sold without consignor
reserves. All lots will open at 50% of the low estimate.

36242

Pair of Royal Minton "Beasts" Commemorating the Royal Wedding of Prince Charles and Lady Diana Spencer in 1981

With maker's stamp inscribed 29 July 1981, The Wedding of HRH the Prince of Wales and Lady Diana Spencer, no. 87 of a Limited Edition of 250

Each designed as a winged stylized lion resting on hind legs, one in white bone china, the other bright red, holding the respective Coats-of-Arms of the House of Spencer and the House of Windsor (figures are incorporated in the coats of arm), on a circular white base, the border enhanced with Royal emblems-6 in. high

Provenance:

Purchased from Hope & Glory, London

Estimate: $3,000 - $5,000

36243

Princess Diana Presentation Carriage Clock

Circa 1995, Hope & Glory Ceramic Specialists, London, retailed by Garrard

The rectangular clock of typical form, with polished gilded brass sides and beveled glass panels, the white enamel dial with black Roman chapters and Arabic designated minute numerals above crowned initial *D* for Diana, Princess of Wales (1961-1997), the reverse inscribed *made in England 11 Jewels*-4 1/4 x 2 7/8 x 2 1/8 in.

Provenance:

Made for Princess Diana for presentation to a single recipient as a personal gift

Purchased from Hope & Glory, London

Estimate: $8,000 - $10,000

The Russo Collection is being sold without consignor reserves. All lots will open at 50% of the low estimate.

Session Two, Auction #5003 | Thursday, April 24, 12:00 PM CT   165

36244

Paragon Prince Charles and Princess Diana Porcelain Wedding Loving Cup

1981

Cylindrical, one side decorated with the British Coat of Arms above the inscription *Ich Dier*, the other side with the portraits of Charles and Diana each within an oval frame below the British Royal Crown and the Prince of Wales Feathers flanked by the Union Jacks and flags of the commonwealth, with the inscriptions *The Prince of Wales and Lady Diana Spencer- Married by the Archbishop of Canterbury, 1981-Royal Wedding, St. Paul's Cathedral, Wednesday, July 29th*, with gilded lion handles-4 7/8 in. high

Provenance:

Purchased from Camden Passage, London

Estimate: $500 - $700

36245

Princess Diana Halcyon Days Porcelain Presentation Box

Oval, overall decorated with pale green lattice design, the sides enhanced with floral enameled garlands, the cover with a central floral wreath enclosing the crowned initial *D* for Diana, Princess of Wales (1961-1997), on white ground with white interior, the base with maker's stamp- 2 3/4 in. wide

Provenance:

Commissioned by Princess Diana as a presentation gift to high-ranking visiting dignitaries or important guests or hosts

Purchased from Hope & Glory, London

Estimate: $3,000 - $5,000

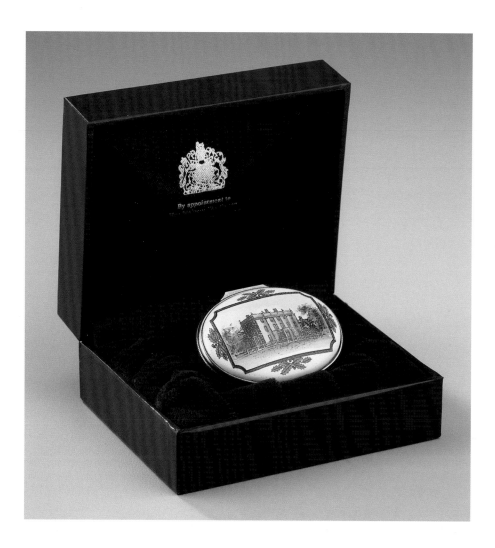

36246

Prince of Wales and Princess Diana Halcyon Days Porcelain Presentation Christmas Box

Oval, the hinged cover decorated with enameled view of Highgrove within a red bracket frame adorned with sprigs of holly or mistletoe, the base of vermillion enamel, opening to reveal inscription *Happy Christmas 1987 from Charles and Diana*, the base with maker's stamp- 2 in. wide

Provenance:

Commissioned by Prince and Princess of Wales as a presentation gift to a close member of the staff, Christmas 1987

Purchased from Hope & Glory, London

Estimate: $3,000 - $4,000

36247

A Substantial Collection of Twenty Prince Charles and Princess Diana Halcyon Days Porcelain Pill Boxes, Each Presented to a Member of their Entourage who Accompanied Them on a Foreign Visit from 1985 to 1993

Circular, each enameled in vibrant colors with representative scene or symbols of the countries visited, the base of each with Halcyon Days maker's stamp-1 1/4 in diam., comprising:

Eleven boxes presented by the Prince of Wales and Princess Diana jointly, each displaying the Prince of Wales Feathers, the interior inscribed *Presented by Their Royal Highnesses The Prince and Princess of Wales* including:

Australia and America, 1985 with Prince of Wales Feathers on white ground with red base

Canada and Japan, 1986 depicting Royal Canadian Mounted Policeman and a Geisha with red base

Vienna, 1986 with Prince of Wales Feathers on white ground below view of Schönbrunn Palace with red base

Oman, Qatar, Bahrain, and Saudi Arabia, November 1986, depicting Arab building with green base

Madrid, 1987 depicting the Prado within a red frame on pale yellow ground

France, 1988 with l'Arc de Triomphe framed within the tricolor with blue base

Hong Kong and Indonesia, 1989 depicting an ancient temple encircled by a Chinese dragon with red base

Nigeria and Cameroon, March 1990 depicting respective flags of the nations on deep blue ground with blue base

Japan, November 1990 depicting Japanese Emperor and his wife with red base

Brazil, April 1991, depicting *Pao de Açucar* in Rio de Janeiro with moss green base

India, February 1992 with view of the Taj Mahal, with green base; this was the famous visit when Diana sat alone in front of the Taj Mahal

Four boxes presented by the Prince of Wales, each displaying the Prince of Wales Feathers, the interior inscribed *Presented by His Royal Highness The Prince of Wales* including:

Texas, California, 1986 depicting the two state flags on white ground with deep blue base

Harvard, Boston, Chicago, 1986 depicting various buildings associated with those locales on burgundy base

Swaziland, Malawi, Kenya, Botswana, April 1987 depicting scenes of an African Safari with pale blue base

New York, Bahamas, Palm Beach, Washington, Puerto Ayacucho, 1989 depicting a stylized map of United States and the Caribbean with blue base

Five boxes presented by the Princess Diana, each displaying a crowned insignia *D* for Diana, Princess of Wales, some within oval frames, the interior inscribed *Presented by Her Royal Highness The Princess of Wales* including:

Lille, Paris, 1992 depicting the Eiffel Tower and an ancient clock tower against blue sky with a red, white, and blue border on deep blue base

Egypt, May 1992, depicting the Nile and various temples in Cairo, Luxor, and Aswan with a red, white, and blue border on deep blue base

Hungary, 1992 depicting a Hungarian castle with patterned border on moss green base

Zimbabwe, July 1993 depicting a map of the country with names of the cities *Harare, Chitungwiza,* and *Masvingo* on earth-colored base

Nepal, 1993, depicting a Hindu temple against blue sky with a red, white, and blue border on deep blue base

Provenance:

Purchased from Hope & Glory, London

Estimate: $35,000 - $45,000

End of Auction

The Russo Collection is being sold without consignor reserves. All lots will open at 50% of the low estimate.

Session Two, Auction #5003 | Thursday, April 24, 12:00 PM CT   169

HERITAGE

IMPORTANT FINE ART AUCTION

MAY 8-9, 2008 • DALLAS, TEXAS • LIVE & ONLINE

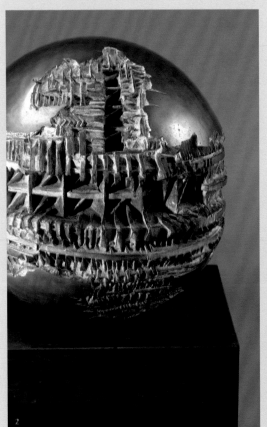

LOT VIEWING:
May 2-3, 5-8

LIVE AUCTION:
May 8-9

To receive a complimentary catalog of your choice, register online at HA.com/CAT8344 or call 866-835-3243 and mention reference #CAT8344. The entire catalog will go online approximately March 17.

1 ALEXANDER CALDER (American 1898-1976)
Untitled, Butterfly on Spiral, 1966
Gouache on paper
22-¾ x 30-⅝ inches (57.8 x 77.8 cm)
Estimate: $20,000-$30,000

2 ARNALDO POMODORO (Italian b. 1926)
Piccolo Sfera
Bronze
20 x 20 inches (50.8 x 50.8 cm)
Estimate: $150,000-$250,000

3 ANDY WARHOL (American 1928-1987)
Jacqueline Kennedy II (Jackie II), 1966
from 11 Pop Artists II, (F. & S. II.14)
Screenprint in colors
24 x 30 inches (61.0 x 76.2 cm)
Estimate: $20,000-$25,000

4 ANDY WARHOL (American 1928-1987)
Jacqueline Kennedy I (Jackie I), 1966
from 11 Pop Artist I, (F. & S. 13)
Screenprint in silver
24 x 20 inches (61.0 x 50.8 cm)
Estimate: $10,000-$15,000

5 ANDY WARHOL (American 1928-1987)
Jacqueline Kennedy III (Jackie III), 1966
from 11 Pop Artists, Volume III (F. & S. II.15)
Screenprint in colors
39-¾ x 30 inches (101.0 x 76.2 cm)
Estimate: $15,000-$20,000

ALWAYS ACCEPTING QUALITY CONSIGNMENTS
of Fine and Decorative Arts, Sculpture, Photography, Western Art, Early Texas Art, and Illustration Art.

FINE SILVER & VERTU AUCTION

MAY 21, 2008 • DALLAS TEXAS • LIVE & ONLINE

The premier auction house for:

- 19th-century American silver
- English silver
- Continental silver
- Russian silver
- American Colonial silver
- Objets de vertu

LOT VIEWING: May 16-21
LIVE AUCTION: May 21

To receive a complimentary catalog of your choice, register online at HA.com/CAT8344 or call 866-835-3243 and mention reference #CAT8344. The entire catalog will go online approximately April 24.

1 **An American Colonial Silver Tankard**
   Richard Van Dyke, New York, New York
   Circa 1750
   Estimate: $40,000-60,000

2 **A Russian Cut Crystal and Silver Punch Bowl with Lid and Ladle**
   Andrei Stepanovich Bragin, St. Petersburg, Russia, circa 1896-1908
   Cut glass, silver and silver gilt
   Estimate: $8,000-$12,000

3 **A Victorian Silver Centerpiece**
   Designed by Edmund Cotterill
   Robert Garrard & Co.
   London, England, 1854
   Estimate: $40,000-60,000

Annual Sales Exceeding $600 Million • Over 350,000 Registered Online Bidder-Members

3500 Maple Ave, 17th Floor • Dallas, Texas 75219 • 214-409-1444 • 800-872-6467 ext. 1444 • HA.com

THE WORLD'S THIRD LARGEST AUCTION HOUSE
HERITAGE HA.com
Auction Galleries

HERITAGE
DECORATIVE ARTS AUCTION

MAY 22, 2008 • DALLAS TEXAS • LIVE & ONLINE

2

3

4

LOT VIEWING:
May 16-21
(Excluding Sunday)
LIVE AUCTION:
May 22

To receive a complimentary catalog of your choice, register online at HA.com/CAT8344 or call 866-835-3243 and mention reference #CAT8344. **The entire catalog will go online approximately April 28.**

1

1 **DALE CHIHULY (American, b. 1941)**
Macchia, 2002
Glass
10 1/2 in. high (26.7 cm.)
Estimate: $8,000-$10,000

2 **A French Gilt Bronze Mounted Porcelain Ewer**
Designed by Agathon Leonard (French, 1841-1923), circa 1900
Porcelain manufactured by Pierre-Adrien Dalpayrat, Bourg-la-Reine, France (1844-1910)
Gilt bronze mounts manufactured by Louchet Frères Foundry, Paris, France
10 3/4 inches (27.3 cm) high
Estimate: $10,000-$15,000

3 **A Napoleon III Bronze and Gilt Bronze Mantle Clock, "Au Taureau"**
France
1852-1870
Bronze and gilt bronze
33 in. high x 27 in. wide (83.8 x 68.6 cm)
Estimate: $15,000-$20,000

4 **A Burgun, Schverer et Cie Cameo Glass Vase**
Meisenthal, France
Circa 1900
10 1/4 in. high (26 cm.)
Estimate: $6,000-8,000

HERITAGE

RUSSIAN FINE & DECORATIVE ART AUCTION

JUNE 4, 2008 • DALLAS, TEXAS • LIVE & ONLINE

LOT VIEWING:
May 30-June 4

LIVE AUCTION:
June 4

NIKOLAI EFIMOVICH TIMKOV
(Russian, 1912-1993)
Rostov in Winter, 1970-74
Oil on canvas
56 x 56 inches (142.2 x 142.2 cm)
Estimate: $200,000-$300,000
From the Kenneth Pushkin Collection

Heritage will continue to seek consignments for this auction until April 2.
For more information contact Dr. Douglass Brown at either 972.834.4056 or douglassb@ha.com

To receive a complimentary copy of this catalog, register online at HA.com/CATA8344 or call 866-835-3243 and mention reference #CATA8344. The entire catalog will go online approximately May 10.

WE ARE ALWAYS ACCEPTING CONSIGNMENTS IN THE FOLLOWING CATEGORIES:Fine & Decorative Arts, Antiques, Rare Coins & Currency, Illustration Art, Comics & Comic Art, Civil War & Americana, American Indian Art, Rare Books & Manuscripts, Entertainment Memorabilia, Jewelry & Timepieces, Natural History, Sports Collectibles, Vintage Movie Posters and Stamps.

Annual Sales Exceeding $600 Million • Over 350,000 Registered Online Bidder-Members
3500 Maple Ave, 17th Floor • Dallas, Texas 75219 • 214.409.1444 • 214.528.3500 ext. 1444 • HA.com

HERITAGE HA.com
Auction Galleries

TX Auctioneer licenses: Samuel Foose: 11727; Scott Peterson: 13256; Robert Korver: 13754; Steve Roach: 16338; Ed Griffith: 16343; Bob Merrill: 13408. This auction is subject to a 19.5% Buyer's Premium.
8344

TERMS AND CONDITIONS OF AUCTION

Auctioneer and Auction:

1. This Auction is presented by Heritage Auction Galleries, a d/b/a/ of Heritage Auctions, Inc., or their affiliates Heritage Numismatic Auctions, Inc., or Heritage Vintage Sports Auctions Inc., or Currency Auctions of America, Inc., as identified with the applicable licensing information on the title page of the catalog or on the HA.com Internet site (the "Auctioneer"). The Auction is conducted under these Terms and Conditions of Auction and applicable state and local law. Announcements and corrections from the podium and those made through the Terms and Conditions of Auctions appearing on the Internet at HA.com supersede those in the printed catalog.

Buyer's Premium:

2. On bids placed through Heritage, a Buyer's Premium of fifteen percent (15%) will be added to the successful hammer price bid on lots in Coin and Currency auctions, or nineteen and one-half percent (19.5%) on lots in all other auctions. If your bid is placed through eBay Live, a Buyer's Premium equal to the normal Buyer's Premium plus an additional five percent (5%) of the hammer price will be added to the successful bid up to a maximum Buyer's Premium of Twenty Two and one-half percent (22.5%). There is a minimum Buyer's Premium of $9.00 per lot. In Gallery Auctions (sealed bid auctions of mostly bulk numismatic material), the Buyer's Premium is 19.5%.

Auction Venues:

3. The following Auctions are conducted solely on the Internet: Heritage Weekly Internet Coin, Currency, Comics, and Vintage Movie Poster Auctions; Heritage Monthly Internet Sports and Marketplace Auctions; Final Sessions. Signature Auctions and Grand Format Auctions accept bids on the Internet first, followed by a floor bidding session; bids may be placed prior to the floor bidding session by Internet, telephone, fax, or mail. Heritage Live and eBay Live provide real time bidding options to registered clients.

Bidders:

4. Any person participating or registering for the Auction agrees to be bound by and accepts these Terms and Conditions of Auction ("Bidder(s)").

5. All Bidders must meet Auctioneer's qualifications to bid. Any Bidder who is not a client in good standing of the Auctioneer may be disqualified at Auctioneer's sole option and will not be awarded lots. Such determination may be made by Auctioneer in its sole and unlimited discretion, at any time prior to, during, or even after the close of the Auction. Auctioneer reserves the right to exclude any person it deems in its sole opinion is disruptive to the Auction or is otherwise commercially unsuitable.

6. If an entity places a bid, then the person executing the bid on behalf of the entity agrees to personally guarantee payment for any successful bid.

Credit:

7. Bidders who have not established credit with the Auctioneer must either furnish satisfactory credit information (including two collectibles-related business references) well in advance of the Auction or supply valid credit card information. Bids placed through our Interactive Internet program will only be accepted from pre-registered Bidders; Bidders who are not members of HA.com or affiliates should pre-register at least two business days before the first session to allow adequate time to contact references. Additionally Bidders who have not previously established credit or who wish to bid in excess of their established credit history may be required to provide their social security number or the last four digits thereof to us so a credit check may be performed prior to Auctioneer's acceptance of a bid.

Bidding Options:

8. Bids in Signature Auctions or Grand Format Auctions may be placed as set forth in the printed catalog section entitled "Choose your bidding method." For auctions held solely on the Internet, see the alternatives on HA.com. Review at HA.com/common/howtobid.php.

9. Presentment of Bids: Non-Internet bids (including but not limited to podium, fax, phone and mail bids) are treated similar to floor bids in that they must be on-increment or at a half increment (called a cut bid). Any podium, fax, phone, or mail bids that do not conform to a full or half increment will be rounded up or down to the nearest full or half increment and this revised amount will be considered your high bid.

10. Auctioneer's Execution of Certain Bids. Auctioneer cannot be responsible for your errors in bidding, so carefully check that every bid is entered correctly. When identical mail or FAX bids are submitted, preference is given to the first received. To ensure the greatest accuracy, your written bids should be entered on the standard printed bid sheet and be received at Auctioneer's place of business at least two business days before the Auction start. Auctioneer is not responsible for executing mail bids or FAX bids received on or after the day the first lot is sold, nor Internet bids submitted after the published closing time; nor is Auctioneer responsible for proper execution of bids submitted by telephone, mail, FAX, e-mail, Internet, or in person once the Auction begins. Internet bids may not be withdrawn until your written request is received and acknowledged by Auctioneer (FAX: 214-4438425); such requests must state the reason, and may constitute grounds for withdrawal of bidding privileges. Lots won by mail Bidders will not be delivered at the Auction unless prearranged.

11. Caveat as to Bid Increments. Bid increments (over the current bid level) determine the lowest amount you may bid on a particular lot. Bids greater than one increment over the current bid can be any whole dollar amount. It is possible under several circumstances for winning bids to be between increments, sometimes only $1 above the previous increment. Please see: "How can I lose by less than an increment?" on our website.

The following chart governs current bidding increments.

Current Bid	Bid Increment	Current Bid	Bid Increment
<$10	$1	$20,000 - $29,999	$2,000
$10 - $29	$2	$30,000 - $49,999	$2,500
$30 - $49	$3	$50,000 - $99,999	$5,000
$50 - $99	$5	$100,000 - $199,999	$10,000
$100 - $199	$10	$200,000 - $299,999	$20,000
$200 - $299	$20	$300,000 - $499,999	$25,000
$300 - $499	$25	$500,000 - $999,999	$50,000
$500 - $999	$50	$1,000,000 - $1,999,999	$100,000
$1,000 - $1,999	$100	$2,000,000 - $2,999,999	$200,000
$2,000 - $2,999	$200	$3,000,000 - $4,999,999	$250,000
$3,000 - $4,999	$250	$5,000,000 - $9,999,999	$500,000
$5,000 - $9,999	$500	>$10,000,000	$1,000,000
$10,000 - $19,999	$1,000		

12. If Auctioneer calls for a full increment, a floor/phone bidder may request Auctioneer to accept a bid at half of the increment ("Cut Bid") which will be that bidders final bid; if the Auctioneer solicits bids other the expected increment, they will not be considered Cut Bids, and bidders accepting such increments may continue to participate.

Conducting the Auction:

13. Notice of the consignor's liberty to place bids on his lots in the Auction is hereby made in accordance with Article 2 of the Texas Uniform Commercial Code. A "Minimum Bid" is an amount below which the lot will not sell. THE CONSIGNOR OF PROPERTY MAY PLACE WRITTEN "Minimum Bids" ON HIS LOTS IN ADVANCE OF THE AUCTION; ON SUCH LOTS, IF THE HAMMER PRICE DOES NOT MEET THE "Minimum Bid", THE CONSIGNOR MAY PAY A REDUCED COMMISSION ON THOSE LOTS. "Minimum Bids" are generally posted online several days prior to the Auction closing. For any successful bid placed by a consignor on his Property on the Auction floor, or by any means during the live session, or after the "Minimum Bid" for an Auction have been posted, we will require the consignor to pay full Buyer's Premium and Seller's Commissions on such lot.

14. The highest qualified Bidder recognized by the Auctioneer shall be the buyer. In the event of any dispute between any Bidders at an Auction, Auctioneer may at his sole discretion reoffer the lot. Auctioneer's decision and declaration of the winning Bidder shall be final and binding upon all Bidders. Bids properly offered, whether by floor Bidder or other means of bidding, may on occasion be missed or go unrecognized; in such cases, the Auctioneer may declare the recognized bid accepted as the winning bid, regardless of whether a competing bid may have been higher.

15. Auctioneer reserves the right to refuse to honor any bid or to limit the amount of any bid which, in his sole discretion, is not submitted in "Good Faith," or is not supported by satisfactory credit, collectibles references, or otherwise. A bid is considered not made in "Good Faith" when an insolvent or irresponsible person, or a person under the age of eighteen makes it. Regardless of the disclosure of his identity, any bid by a consignor or his agent on a lot consigned by him is deemed to be made in "Good Faith." Any person apparently appearing on the OFAC list is not eligible to bid.

16. Nominal Bids. The Auctioneer in its sole discretion may reject nominal bids, small opening bids, or very nominal advances. If a lot bearing estimates fails to open for 40 –60% of the low estimate, the Auctioneer may pass the item or may place a protective bid on behalf of the consignor.

17. Lots bearing bidding estimates shall open at Auctioneer's discretion (approximately 50% of the low estimate). In the event that no bid meets or exceeds that opening amount, the lot shall pass as unsold.

18. All items are to be purchased per lot as numerically indicated and no lots will be broken. Bids will be accepted in whole dollar amounts only. No "buy" or "unlimited" bids will be accepted. Off-increment bids may be accepted by the Auctioneer at Signature Auctions and Grand Format Auctions. Auctioneer reserves the right to withdraw, prior to the close, any lots from the Auction.

19. Auctioneer reserves the right to rescind the sale in the event of nonpayment, breach of a warranty, disputed ownership, auctioneer's clerical error or omission in exercising bids and reserves, or otherwise. In cases of nonpayment, Auctioneer's election to void a sale does not relieve the Bidder from their obligation to pay Auctioneer its fees (seller's and buyer's premium) and any other damages or expenses pertaining to the lot.

20. Auctioneer occasionally experiences Internet and/or Server service outages during which Bidders cannot participate or place bids. If such outage occurs, we may at our discretion extend bidding for the auction. This policy applies only to widespread outages and not to isolated problems that occur in various parts of the country from time to time. Auctioneer periodically schedules system downtime for maintenance and other purposes, which may be covered by the Outage Policy. Bidders unable to place their Bids through the Internet are directed to bid through Client Services at 1-800-872-6467.

21. The Auctioneer or its affiliates may consign items to be sold in the Auction, and may bid on those lots or any other lots. Auctioneer or affiliates expressly reserve the right to modify any such bids at any time prior to the hammer based upon data made known to the Auctioneer or its affiliates. The Auctioneer may extend advances, guarantees, or loans to certain consignors, and may extend financing or other credits at varying rates to certain Bidders in the auction.

22. The Auctioneer has the right to sell certain unsold items after the close of the Auction. Such lots shall be considered sold during the Auction and all these Terms and Conditions shall apply to such sales including but not limited to the Buyer's Premium, return rights, and disclaimers.

Payment:

23. All sales are strictly for cash in United States dollars. Cash includes: U.S. currency, bank wire, cashier checks, travelers checks, eChecks, and bank money orders, all subject to reporting requirements. Checks may be subject to clearing before delivery of the purchases. Heritage reserves the right to determine if a check constitutes "good funds" when drawn on a U.S. bank for ten days, and thirty days when drawn on an international bank. Credit Card (Visa or Master Card only) and PayPal payments may be accepted up to $10,000 from non-dealers at the sole discretion of the auctioneer, subject to the following limitations: a) sales are only to the cardholder, b) purchases are shipped to the cardholder's registered and verified address, c) Auctioneer may pre-approve the cardholder's credit line, d) a credit card transaction may not be used in conjunction with any other financing or extended terms offered by the Auctioneer, and must transact immediately upon invoice presentation, e) rights of return are governed by these Terms and Conditions, which supersede those conditions promulgated by the card issuer, f) floor Bidders must present their card.

24. Payment is due upon closing of the Auction session, or upon presentment of an invoice. Auctioneer reserves the right to void an invoice if payment in full is not received within 7 days after the close of the Auction. In cases of nonpayment, Auctioneer's election to void a sale does not relieve the Bidder from their obligation to pay Auctioneer its fees (seller's and buyer's premium) on the lot and any other damages pertaining to the lot.

25. Lots delivered in the States of Texas, California, or other states where the Auction may be held, are subject to all applicable state and local taxes, unless appropriate permits are on file with us. Bidder agrees to pay Auctioneer the actual amount of tax due in the event that sales tax is not properly collected due to: 1) an expired, inaccurate, inappropriate tax certificate or declaration, 2) an incorrect interpretation of the applicable statute, 3) or any other reason. The appropriate form or certificate must be on file at and verified by Heritage five days prior to Auction or tax must be paid; only if such form or certificate is received by Heritage within 4 days of the Auction can a tax refund be made. Lots from different Auctions may not be aggregated for sales tax purposes.

26. In the event that a Bidder's payment is dishonored upon presentment(s), Bidder shall pay the maximum statutory processing fee set by applicable state law. If you attempt to pay via eCheck and your financial institution denies this transfer from your bank account, or the payment cannot be completed using the selected funding source, you agree to complete payment using your credit card on file.

27. If any Auction invoice submitted by Auctioneer is not paid in full when due, the unpaid balance will bear interest at the highest rate permitted by law from the date of invoice until paid. If the Auctioneer refers any invoice to an attorney for collection, the buyer agrees to pay attorney's fees, court costs, and other collection costs incurred by Auctioneer. If the Auctioneer assigns collection to its in-house legal staff, such attorney's time expended on the matter shall be compensated at a rate comparable to the hourly rate of independent attorneys.

28. In the event a successful Bidder fails to pay all amounts due, Auctioneer reserves the right to resell the merchandise, and such Bidder agrees to pay for the reasonable costs of resale, including a 10% seller's commission, and also to pay any difference between the resale price and the price of the previously successful bid. Auctioneer may sell the merchandise to an under Bidder or at private sale and in such case the Bidder shall be responsible for any deficiency between the original and subsequent sale.

29. Auctioneer reserves the right to require payment in full in good funds before delivery of the merchandise.

30. Auctioneer shall have a lien against the merchandise purchased by the buyer to secure payment of the Auction invoice. Auctioneer is further granted a lien and the right to retain possession of any other property of the buyer then held by the Auctioneer or its affiliates to secure payment of any Auction invoice or any other amounts due the Auctioneer or affiliates from the buyer. With respect to these lien rights, Auctioneer shall have all the rights of a secured creditor under Article 9 of the Texas Uniform Commercial Code, including but not limited to the right of sale. In addition, with respect to payment of the Auction invoice(s), the buyer waives any and all rights of offset he might otherwise have against the Auctioneer and the consignor of the merchandise included on the invoice. If a Bidder owes Auctioneer or its affiliates on any account, Auctioneer and its affiliates shall have the right to offset such unpaid account by any credit balance due Bidder, and it may secure by possessory lien any unpaid amount by any of the Bidder's property in their possession.

31. Title shall not pass to the successful Bidder until all invoices are paid in full. It is the responsibility of the buyer to provide adequate insurance coverage for the items once they have been delivered.

Delivery; Shipping; and Handling Charges:

32. Shipping and handling charges will be added to invoices. Please refer to Auctioneer's website www. HA.com/common/shipping.php for the latest charges or call Auctioneer. Auctioneer is unable to combine purchases from other auctions or affiliates into one package for shipping purposes. Lots won will be shipped in a commercially reasonable time after payment in good funds for the merchandise and the shipping fees is received or credit extended, except when third-party shipment occurs.

33. Successful international Bidders shall provide written shipping instructions, including specified customs declarations, to the Auctioneer for any lots to be delivered outside of the United States. NOTE: Declaration value shall be the item'(s) hammer price together with its buyer's premium and Auctioneer shall use the correct harmonized code for the lot. Domestic Buyers on lots designated for third-party shipment must designate the common carrier, accept risk of loss, and prepay shipping costs.

34. All shipping charges will be borne by the successful Bidder. Any risk of loss during shipment will be borne by the buyer following Auctioneer's delivery to the designated common carrier or third-party shipper, regardless of domestic or foreign shipment.

35. Due to the nature of some items sold, it shall be the responsibility for the successful Bidder to arrange pick-up and shipping through third-parties; as to such items Auctioneer shall have no liability. Failure to pick-up or arrange shipping in a timely fashion (within ten days) shall subject Lots to storage and moving charges, including a $100 administration fee plus $10 daily storage. In the event the Lot is not removed within ninety days, the Lot may be offered for sale to recover any past due storage or moving fees, including a 10% Seller's Fee.

36. The laws of various countries regulate the import or export of certain plant and animal properties, including (but not limited to) items made of (or including) ivory, whalebone, turtleshell, coral, crocodile, or other wildlife. Transport of such lots may require special licenses for export, import, or both. Bidder is responsible for: 1) obtaining all information on such restricted items for both export and import; 2) obtaining all such licenses and/or permits. Delay or failure to obtain any such license or permit does not relieve the buyer of timely compliance with standard payment terms. For further information, please contact Bill Taylor at 800-872-6467 ext. 1280.

37. Any request for shipping verification for undelivered packages must be made within 30 days of shipment by Auctioneer.

Cataloging, Warranties and Disclaimers:

38. NO WARRANTY, WHETHER EXPRESSED OR IMPLIED, IS MADE WITH RESPECT TO ANY DESCRIPTION CONTAINED IN THIS AUCTION OR ANY SECOND OPINE. Any description of the items or second opine contained in this Auction is for the sole purpose of identifying the items for those Bidders who do not have the opportunity to view the lots prior to bidding, and no description of items has been made part of the basis of the bargain or has created any express warranty that the goods would conform to any description made by Auctioneer. Color variations can be expected in any electronic or printed imaging, and are not grounds for the return of any lot.

39. Auctioneer is selling only such right or title to the items being sold as Auctioneer may have by virtue of consignment agreements on the date of auction and disclaims any warranty of title to the Property. Auctioneer disclaims any warranty of merchantability or fitness for any particular purposes. All images, descriptions, sales data, and archival records are the exclusive property of Auctioneer, and may be used by Auctioneer for advertising, promotion, archival records, and any other uses deemed appropriate.

40. Translations of foreign language documents may be provided as a convenience to interested parties. Heritage makes no representation as to the accuracy of those translations and will not be held responsible for errors in bidding arising from inaccuracies in translation.

41. Auctioneer disclaims all liability for damages, consequential or otherwise, arising out of or in connection with the sale of any Property by Auctioneer to Bidder. No third party may rely on any benefit of these Terms and Conditions and any rights, if any, established hereunder are personal to the Bidder and may not be assigned. Any statement made by the Auctioneer is an opinion and does not constitute a warranty or representation. No employee of Auctioneer may alter these Terms and Conditions, and, unless signed by a principal of Auctioneer, any such alteration is null and void.

42. Auctioneer shall not be liable for breakage of glass or damage to frames (patent or latent); such defects, in any event, shall not be a basis for any claim for return or reduction in purchase price.

Release:

43. In consideration of participation in the Auction and the placing of a bid, Bidder expressly releases Auctioneer, its officers, directors and employees, its affiliates, and its outside experts that provide second opines, from any and all claims, cause of action, chose of action, whether at law or equity or any arbitration or mediation rights existing under the rules of any professional society or affiliation based upon the assigned description, or a derivative theory, breach of warranty express or implied, representation or other matter set forth within these Terms and Conditions of Auction or otherwise. In the event of a claim, Bidder agrees that such rights and privileges conferred therein are strictly construed as specifically declared herein; e.g., authenticity, typographical error, etc. and are the exclusive remedy. Bidder, by non-compliance to these express terms of a granted remedy, shall waive any claim against Auctioneer.

44. Notice: Some Property sold by Auctioneer are inherently dangerous e.g. firearms, cannons, and small items that may be swallowed or ingested or may have latent defects all of which may cause harm to a person. Purchaser accepts all risk of loss or damage from its purchase of these items and

Auctioneer disclaims any liability whether under contract or tort for damages and losses, direct or inconsequential, and expressly disclaims any warranty as to safety or usage of any lot sold.

Dispute Resolution and Arbitration Provision:

45. By placing a bid or otherwise participating in the auction, Bidder accepts these Terms and Conditions of Auction, and specifically agrees to the alternative dispute resolution provided herein. Arbitration replaces the right to go to court, including the right to a jury trial.

46. Auctioneer in no event shall be responsible for consequential damages, incidental damages, compensatory damages, or other damages arising from the auction of any lot. In the event that Auctioneer cannot deliver the lot or subsequently it is established that the lot lacks title, or other transfer or condition issue is claimed, Auctioneer's liability shall be limited to rescission of sale and refund of purchase price; in no case shall Auctioneer's maximum liability exceed the high bid on that lot, which bid shall be deemed for all purposes the value of the lot. After one year has elapsed, Auctioneer's maximum liability shall be limited to any commissions and fees Auctioneer earned on that lot.

47. In the event of an attribution error, Auctioneer may at its sole discretion, correct the error on the Internet, or, if discovered at a later date, to refund the buyer's purchase price without further obligation.

48. Arbitration Clause: All controversies or claims under this Agreement or arising from or pertaining to: this Agreement or related documents, or to the Properties consigned hereunder, or the enforcement or interpretation hereof of this or any related agreements, or damage to Properties, payment, or any other matter, or because of an alleged breach, default or misrepresentation under the provisions hereof or otherwise, that cannot be settled amicably within one (1) month from the date of notification of either party to the other of such dispute or question, which notice shall specify the details of such dispute or question, shall be settled by final and binding arbitration by one arbitrator appointed by the American Arbitration Association ("AAA"). The arbitration shall be conducted in Dallas, Dallas County, Texas in accordance with the then existing Commercial Arbitration Rules of the AAA. The arbitration shall be brought within two (2) years of the alleged breach, default or misrepresentation or the claim is waived. The prevailing party (a party that is awarded substantial and material relief on its claim or defense) may be awarded its reasonable attorney's fees and costs. Judgment upon the award rendered by the arbitrator may be entered in any court having jurisdiction thereof; provided, however, that the law applicable to any controversy shall be the law of the State of Texas, regardless of its or any other jurisdiction's choice of law principles and under the provisions of the Federal Arbitration Act.

49. No claims of any kind can be considered after the settlements have been made with the consignors. Any dispute after the settlement date is strictly between the Bidder and consignor without involvement or responsibility of the Auctioneer.

50. In consideration of their participation in or application for the Auction, a person or entity (whether the successful Bidder, a Bidder, a purchaser and/or other Auction participant or registrant) agrees that all disputes in any way relating to, arising under, connected with, or incidental to these Terms and Conditions and purchases, or default in payment thereof, shall be arbitrated pursuant to the arbitration provision. In the event that any matter including actions to compel arbitration, construe the agreement, actions in aid or arbitration or otherwise needs to be litigated, such litigation shall be exclusively in the Courts of the State of Texas, in Dallas County, Texas, and if necessary the corresponding appellate courts. The successful Bidder, purchaser, or Auction participant also expressly submits himself to the personal jurisdiction of the State of Texas.

51. These Terms & Conditions provide specific remedies for occurrences in the auction and delivery process. Where such remedies are afforded, they shall be interpreted strictly. Bidder agrees that any claim shall utilize such remedies; Bidder making a claim in excess of those remedies provided in these Terms and Conditions agrees that in no case whatsoever shall Auctioneer's maximum liability exceed the high bid on that lot, which bid shall be deemed for all purposes the value of the lot.

Miscellaneous:

52. Agreements between Bidders and consignors to effectuate a non-sale of an item at Auction, inhibit bidding on a consigned item to enter into a private sale agreement for said item, or to utilize the Auctioneer's Auction to obtain sales for non-selling consigned items subsequent to the Auction, are strictly prohibited. If a subsequent sale of a previously consigned item occurs in violation of this provision, Auctioneer reserves the right to charge Bidder the applicable Buyer's Premium and consignor a Seller's Commission as determined for each auction venue and by the terms of the seller's agreement.

53. Acceptance of these Terms and Conditions qualifies Bidder as a Heritage customer who has consented to be contacted by Heritage in the future. In conformity with "do-not-call" regulations promulgated by the Federal or State regulatory agencies, participation by the Bidder is affirmative consent to being contacted at the phone number shown in his application and this consent shall remain in effect until it is revoked in writing. Heritage may from time to time contact Bidder concerning sale, purchase, and auction opportunities available through Heritage and its affiliates and subsidiaries.

54. Rules of Construction: Auctioneer presents properties in a number of collectible fields. As such, specific venues have promulgated supplemental Terms and Conditions for that venue. Nothing herein shall be construed to waive the general Terms and Conditions of Auction by these additional rules and shall be construed to give force and effect to the rules in their entirety.

State Notices:

Notice as to an Auction in California. Auctioneer has in compliance with Title 2.95 of the California Civil Code as amended October 11, 1993 Sec. 1812.600, posted with the California Secretary of State its bonds for it and its employees, and the auction is being conducted in compliance with Sec. 2338 of the Commercial Code and Sec. 535 of the Penal Code.

Notice as to an Auction in New York City. These Terms and Conditions are designed to conform to the applicable sections of the New York City Department of Consumer Affairs Rules and Regulations as Amended. This is a Public Auction Sale conducted by Auctioneer. The New York City licensed Auctioneers are Kathleen Guzman, No.0762165, and Samuel W. Foose, No.0952360, who will conduct the Auction on behalf of Heritage Auctions, Inc. ("Auctioneer"). All lots are subject to: the consignor's right to bid thereon in accord with these Terms and Conditions of Auction, consignor's option to receive advances on their consignments, and Auctioneer, in its sole discretion, may offer limited extended financing to registered bidders, in accord with Auctioneer's internal credit standards. A registered bidder may inquire whether a lot is subject to an advance or reserve. Auctioneer has made advances to various consignors in this sale.

Notice as to an Auction in Texas. In compliance with TDLR rule 67.100(c)(1), notice is hereby provided that this auction is covered by a Recovery Fund administered by the Texas Department of Licensing and Regulation, P.O. Box 12157, Austin, Texas 78711 (512) 463-6599. Any complaints may be directed to the same address.

Rev. 3_20_08

Additional Terms & Conditions:
FINE & DECORATIVE ARTS AUCTIONS

FINE AND DECORATIVE ARTS TERM A: LIMITED WARRANTY: Auctioneer warrants authorship, period or culture of each lot sold in this catalog as set out in the BOLD faced type heading in the catalog description of the lot, with the following exclusions. This warranty does not apply to:

i.   authorship of any paintings, drawings or sculpture created prior to 1870, unless the lot is determined to be a counterfeit which has a value at the date of the claim for rescission which is materially less than the purchase price paid for the lot; or

ii. any catalog description where it was specifically mentioned that there is a conflict of specialist opinion on the authorship of a lot; or

iii. authorship which on the date of sale was in accordance with the then generally accepted opinion of scholars and specialists, despite the subsequent discovery of new information, whether historical or physical, concerning the artist or craftsman, his students, school, workshop or followers; or

iv. the identification of periods or dates of execution which may be proven inaccurate by means of scientific processes not generally accepted for use until after publication of the catalog, or which were unreasonably expensive or impractical to use at the time of publication of the catalog.

The term counterfeit is defined as a modern fake or forgery, made less than fifty years ago with the intent to deceive. The authenticity of signatures, monograms, initials or other similar indications of authorship is expressly excluded as a controlling factor in determining whether a work is a counterfeit under the meaning of these Terms and Conditions of Auction.

FINE AND DECORATIVE ARTS TERM B: GLOSSARY OF TERMS

Terms used in this catalog have the following meanings. Please note that all statements in this catalog regarding authorship, attribution, origin, date, age, provenance and condition are statements of opinion and are not treated as a statement of fact.

1.   THOMAS MORAN
     In our opinion, the work is by the artist.

2.   ATTRIBUTED TO THOMAS MORAN
     In our opinion, the work is of the period of the artist which may be whole or in part the work of the artist.

3.   STUDIO, (CIRCLE OR WORKSHOP) OF THOMAS MORAN
     In our opinion, the work is of the period and closely relates to his style.

4.   SCHOOL OF THOMAS MORAN
     In our opinion, the work is by a pupil or a follower of the artist.

5.   MANNER OF THOMAS MORAN
     In our opinion, the work is in the style of the artist and is of a later period.

6.   AFTER THOMAS MORAN
     In our opinion, this work is a copy of the artist.

7.   ASCRIBED TO THOMAS MORAN
     In our opinion, this work is not by the artist, however, previous scholarship has noted this to be a work by the artist.

8.   SIGNED (OR DATED)
     The work has a signature (or date) which is in our opinion is genuine.

9.   BEARS SIGNATURE (OR DATE)
     The work has a signature (or date) which in our opinion is not authentic.

FINE AND DECORATIVE ARTS TERM C: PRESENTMENT: The warranty as to authorship is provided for a period of one (1) year from the date of the auction and is only for the benefit of the original purchaser of record and is not transferable.

FINE AND DECORATIVE ARTS TERM D: The Auction is not on approval. Under extremely limited circumstances not including authenticity (e.g. gross cataloging error), a purchaser who did not bid from the floor may request Auctioneer to evaluate voiding a sale; such request must be made in writing detailing the alleged gross error, and submission of the lot to Auctioneer must be pre-approved by Auctioneer. A bidder must notify the appropriate department head (check the inside front cover of the catalog or our website for a listing of department heads) in writing of the purchaser's request within three (3) days of the non-floor bidder's receipt of the lot. Any lot that is to be evaluated for return must be received in our offices within 30 days after Auction. AFTER THAT 30 DAY PERIOD, NO LOT MAY BE RETURNED FOR ANY REASONS. Lots returned must be in the same condition as when sold and must include any Certificate of Authenticity. No lots purchased by floor bidders may be returned (including those bidders acting as agents for others). Late remittance for purchases may be considered just cause to revoke all return privileges.

FINE AND DECORATIVE ARTS TERM E: The catalog descriptions are provided for identification purposes only. Bidders who intend to challenge a bold-faced provision in the description of a lot must notify Auctioneer in writing within thirty (30) days of the Auction's conclusion. In the event Auctioneer cannot deliver the lot or subsequently it is established that the lot lacks title or the bold faced section of description is incorrect, or other transfer or condition issue is claimed, Auctioneer's liability shall be limited to rescission of sale and refund of purchase price; in no case shall Auctioneer's maximum liability exceed the successful bid on that lot, which bid shall be deemed for all purposes the value of the lot. After one year has elapsed, Auctioneer's maximum liability shall be limited to any commissions and fees Auctioneer earned on that lot.

FINE AND DECORATIVE ARTS TERM F: Any claim as to authorship, provenance, authenticity, or other matter under the remedies provided in the Fine Arts Terms and Conditions or otherwise must be first transmitted to Auctioneer by credible and definitive evidence within the claim period and the opine of two qualified third party experts. The claim must be presented in accord with the remedies provided herein and is subject to the limitations and restrictions provided (including within the described time limitations). Regardless of Purchaser's submissions there is no assurance after such presentment that Auctioneer will validate the claim. Authentication is not an exact science and contrary opinions may not be recognized by Auctioneer. Even if Auctioneer agrees with the contrary opinion of such authentication and provides a remedy within these Terms and Conditions or otherwise, our liability for reimbursement for bidder's third party opines shall not exceed $500. The right of rescission, return, or any other remedy provided in these Terms and Conditions, or any other applicable law, does not extend to authorship of any lot which at the date of Auction was in accordance with the then generally accepted opinion of scholars and specialists, despite the subsequent discovery of new information, whether historical or physical, concerning the artist, his students, school, workshop or followers. Purchaser by placing a bid expressly waives any claim or damage based on such subsequent information as described herein. It is specifically understood that any refund agreed to by the Auctioneer would be limited to the purchase price.

FINE AND DECORATIVE ARTS TERM G: Provenance and authenticity are guaranteed by neither the consignor nor Auctioneer. While every effort is made to determine provenance and authenticity, it is the responsibility of the Bidder to arrive at their own conclusion prior to bidding.

FINE AND DECORATIVE ARTS TERM H: On the fall of Auctioneer's hammer, Buyers of Fine Arts and Decorative Arts lots assumes full risk and responsibility for lot, including shipment by common carrier or third-party shipper, and must provide their own insurance coverage for shipments.

FINE AND DECORATIVE ARTS TERM I: Auctioneer complies with all Federal and State rules and regulations relating to the purchasing, registration and shipping of firearms. A purchaser is required to provide appropriate documents and the payment of associated fees, if any. Purchaser is responsible for providing a shipping address that is suitable for the receipt of a firearm.

WIRING INSTRUCTIONS:
Bank Information: JP Morgan Chase Bank, N.A., 270 Park Avenue, New York, NY 10017
Account Name: HERITAGE NUMISMATIC AUCTIONS MASTER ACCOUNT
ABA Number: 021000021
Account Number: 1884827674
Swift Code: CHASUS33

Interactive Internet™ Bidding

You can now bid with Heritage's exclusive *Interactive Internet™* program, available only at our web site: HA.com. It's fun, and it's easy!

1. Register online at: **HA.com**

2. View the full-color photography of every single lot in the online catalog!

3. Construct your own personal catalog for preview.

4. View the current opening bids on lots you want; review the prices realized archive.

5. Bid and receive immediate notification if you are the top bidder; later, if someone else bids higher, you will be notified automatically by e-mail.

6. The *Interactive Internet™* program opens the lot on the floor at one increment over the second highest bid. As the high bidder, your secret maximum bid will compete for you during the floor auction, and it is possible that you may be outbid on the floor after Internet bidding closes. Bid early, as the earliest bird wins in the event of a tie bid.

7. After the sale, you will be notified of your success. It's that easy!

Bid Live using *HERITAGE LIVE*

This auction is **"HA.com/Live Enabled"** and has continuous bidding from the time the auction is posted on our site through the live event. **When normal Internet bidding ends, visit HA.com/Live and continue to place Live Proxy bids.** When the item hits the auction block, you can continue to bid live against the floor and other live bidders.

Interactive Internet™ Bidding Instructions

1. **Log Onto Website**

   Log onto **HA.com** and chose the portal you're interested in (i.e., coins, comics, movie posters, fine arts, etc.).

2. **Search for Lots**

   Search or browse for the lot you are interested in. You can do this from the home page, from the Auctions home page, or from the home page for the particular auction in which you wish to participate.

3. **Select Lots**

   Click on the link or the photo icon for the lot you want to bid on.

4. **Enter Bid**

   At the top of the page, next to a small picture of the item, is a box outlining the current bid. Enter the amount of your secret maximum bid in the textbox next to "Secret Maximum Bid." The secret maximum bid is the maximum amount you are willing to pay for the item you are bidding on (for more information about bidding and bid increments, please see the section labeled "Bidding Increments" elsewhere in this catalog). Click on the button marked "Place Absentee Bid." A new area on the same page will open up for you to enter your username (or e-mail address) and password. Enter these, then click "Place Absentee Bid" again.

5. **Confirm Absentee Bid**

   You are taken to a page labeled, "Please Confirm Your Bid." This page shows you the name of the item you're bidding on, the current bid, and the maximum bid. When you are satisfied that all the information shown is correct, click on the button labeled, "Confirm Bid."

6. **Bidding Status Notification**

   One of two pages is now displayed.

   a. If your bid is the current high bid, you will be notified and given additional information as to what might happen to affect your high bidder status over the course of the remainder of the auction. You will also receive a Bid Confirmation notice via email.

   b. If your bid is not the current high bid, you will be notified of that fact and given the opportunity to increase your bid.

Mail Bidding at Auction

Mail bidding at auction is fun and easy and only requires a few simple steps.

1. Look through the catalog, and determine the lots of interest.

2. Research their market value by checking price lists and other price guidelines.

3. Fill out your bid sheet, entering your maximum bid on each lot.

4. Verify your bids!

5. Mail Early. Preference is given to the first bids received in case of a tie. When bidding by mail, you frequently purchase items at less than your maximum bid.

Bidding is opened at the published increment above the second highest mail or Internet bid; we act on your behalf as the highest mail bidder. If bidding proceeds, we act as your agent, bidding in increments over the previous bid. This process is continued until you are awarded the lot or you are outbid.

An example of this procedure: You submit a bid of $100, and the second highest mail bid is at $50. Bidding starts at $55 on your behalf. If no other bids are placed, you purchase the lot for $55. If other bids are placed, we bid for you in the posted increments until we reach your maximum bid of $100. If bidding passes your maximum: if you are bidding through the Internet, we will contact you by e-mail; if you bid by mail, we take no other action. Bidding continues until the final bidder wins.

Telephone Bidding

To participate by telephone, please make arrangements by Wednesday, April 23, 2008, 5:00 PM CT with Client Services, Toll Free 866-835-3243.

We strongly recommend that you place preliminary bids by mail, fax, or Internet, even if you intend to participate by telephone. On many occasions this dual approach has helped reduce disappointments due to telephone problems, unexpected travel, late night sessions and time zone differences, etc. We will make sure that you do not bid against yourself.

Mail Bidding Instructions

1. **Name, Address, City, State, Zip**
   Your address is needed to mail your purchases. We need your telephone number to communicate any problems or changes that may affect your bids.

2. **References**
   If you have not established credit with us from previous auctions, you must send a 25% deposit, or list dealers with whom you have credit established.

3. **Lot Numbers and Bids**
   List all lots you desire to purchase. On the reverse are additional columns; you may also use another sheet. Under "Amount" enter the maximum you would pay for that lot (whole dollar amounts only). We will purchase the lot(s) for you as much below your bids as possible.

4. **Total Bid Sheet**
   Add up all bids and list that total in the appropriate box.

5. **Sign Your Bid Sheet**
   By signing the bid sheet, you have agreed to abide by the Terms of Auction listed in the auction catalog.

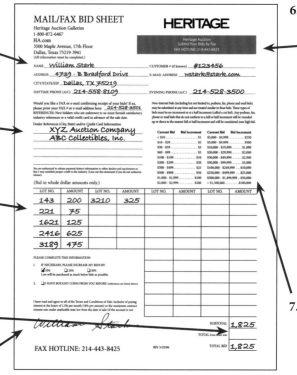

6. **Fax Your Bid Sheet**
   When time is short submit a Mail Bid Sheet on our exclusive Fax Hotline. There's no faster method to get your bids to us *instantly*. Simply use the **Heritage Fax Hotline number: 214-443-8425**.

   When you send us your original after faxing, mark it "Confirmation of Fax" (preferably in red!)

7. **Bidding Increments**
   To facilitate bidding, please consult the Bidding Increments chart in the Terms & Conditions.

The official prices realized list that accompanies our auction catalogs is reserved for bidders and consignors only. We are happy to mail one to others upon receipt of $1.00. Written requests should be directed to Customer Service.

Upcoming Auctions

HERITAGE HA.com
Auction Galleries

HA.com/Consign
Call Our Consignment Hotline
Toll Free: 800-872-6467 Ext. 1444

Over 350,000 Online Registered Bidder-Members • Annual Sales Exceeding $600 Million

United States Coin Auctions	Location	Auction Dates	Consignment Deadline
C.S.N.S.	Rosemont, IL	April 16-19, 2008	Closed
Long Beach	Long Beach, CA	May 28-31, 2008	April 17, 2008
World Coin Auctions	**Location**	**Auction Dates**	**Consignment Deadline**
Long Beach	Long Beach, CA	May 29-31, 2008	April 10, 2008
Long Beach	Long Beach, CA	September 17-20, 2008	July 31, 2008
Currency Auctions	**Location**	**Auction Dates**	**Consignment Deadline**
C.S.N.S.	Rosemont, IL	April 17-19, 2008	Closed
Long Beach	Long Beach, CA	September 19–20, 2008	July 31, 2008
Medals & Tokens	**Location**	**Auction Dates**	**Consignment Deadline**
Long Beach	Long Beach, CA	September 19–20, 2008	August 11, 2008
Fine & Decorative Arts	**Location**	**Auction Dates**	**Consignment Deadline**
Decorative Arts - The Russo Collection	Dallas, TX	April 24, 2008	Closed
Fine Art	Dallas, TX	May 8-9, 2008	Closed
Fine Silver & Vertu	Dallas, TX	May 21, 2008	Closed
Decorative Arts	Dallas, TX	May 22, 2008	Closed
Russian Fine Art	Dallas, TX	June 4, 2008	April 2, 2008
Jewelry & Timepieces Auction	**Location**	**Auction Dates**	**Consignment Deadline**
Estate Jewelry & Timepieces	Dallas, TX	May 20, 2008	March 28, 2008
Jewelry & Time Pieces	Dallas, TX	Dec. 2, 2008	October 10, 2008
Vintage Movie Posters Auctions	**Location**	**Auction Dates**	**Consignment Deadline**
Vintage Movie Posters	Dallas, TX	July 11-12, 2008	May 19, 2008
Comics Auctions	**Location**	**Auction Dates**	**Consignment Deadline**
Illustration Art	Dallas, TX	June 5, 2008	April 20, 2008
Comics & Original Comic Art	Dallas, TX	May 21-23, 2008	April 7, 2008
Music & Entertainment Memorabilia Auctions	**Location**	**Auction Dates**	**Consignment Deadline**
Music, Celebrity & Hollywood Memorabilia	Dallas, TX	April 4-6, 2008	Closed
Music, Celebrity & Hollywood Memorabilia	Dallas, TX	October 4-5, 2008	August 12, 2008
Political Memorabilia & Americana Grand Format Auctions	**Location**	**Auction Dates**	**Consignment Deadline**
Grand Format Americana Auction	Dallas, TX	May 4-5, 2008	Closed
Rare Books & Manuscripts	Dallas, TX	June 3-4, 2008	April 11, 2008
Civil War Auction	Gettysburg, PA	June 29,30, 2008	April 23, 2008
Sports Collectibles Auctions	**Location**	**Auction Dates**	**Consignment Deadline**
Vintage Sports Collectibles & Memorabilia	Dallas, TX	May 3, 2008	Closed
Vintage Sports Collectibles & Memorabilia	Dallas, TX	October 11, 2008	August 19, 2008
Natural History Auctions	**Location**	**Auction Dates**	**Consignment Deadline**
Natural History Auction	Dallas, TX	June 8, 2008	Closed

HERITAGE TUESDAY INTERNET COIN AUCTIONS • HERITAGE SUNDAY INTERNET COIN AUCTIONS • Begin and end every Tuesday and Sunday at 10 PM CT.
HERITAGE TUESDAY INTERNET CURRENCY AUCTIONS • Begin and end every Tuesday at 10 PM CT.
HERITAGE WEEKLY INTERNET COMICS AUCTIONS • Begin and end every Sunday at 10 PM CT.
HERITAGE WEEKLY INTERNET MOVIE POSTER AUCTIONS • Begin and end every Sunday at 10 PM CT.
HERITAGE WEEKLY INTERNET SPORTS AUCTIONS • Begin and end every Sunday at 9 PM CT, with extended bidding available.
HERITAGE MONTHLY MARKETPLACE AUCTIONS • Wednesdays/Thursdays between 4 PM and 10 PM CT. This Auction has a combination of lots consisting of Americana, Sports, Comics, Fine Art/Decorative Arts, Texas Art, Jewelry and Music Memorabilia lots.

3/06/08